P9-CEJ-604

HOME LIFE

A JOURNEY

THROUGH ROOMS

AND

RECOLLECTIONS

suzanne fox

simon & schuster

SIMON & SCHUSTER
Rockefeller Center
1230 Avenue of the Americas
New York, NY 10020

Designed by Jeanette Olender
Manufactured in the United States of America

1   3   5   7   9   10   8   6   4   2

Library of Congress Cataloging-in-Publication Data
Fox, Suzanne.
Home life: a journey through rooms and recollections / Suzanne Fox.
p. cm.
Includes bibliographical references.
1. Fox, Suzanne—Homes and haunts—United States. 2. Women—United
States—Biography. 3. Home—United States. 4. Rooms.
I. Title
HQ 1413. F68A3   1997
304.23—dc21   97-15213   CIP
ISBN 0-684-83517-7

FOR

saul and patricia fox

Contents

HOME LIFE

Introduction

In the bottom of my closet sits a big cardboard box of mementos, a carton I ignore until, every other year or so, I'm overtaken by a bout of curiosity or nostalgia. Inside the carton there are snapshots of my grandfather standing on the porch of his house at the Jersey shore, of an eighteenth-century period room at the Metropolitan Museum of Art, of the Victorian dollhouse I made as a child, of two close friends squinting in the sunny living room of their Los Angeles apartment. A high school essay on my mother's kitchen, a college term paper about Vermeer's luminous interiors, a graduate school oral report I wrote on rooms in the works of Virginia Woolf and Oscar Wilde. A single blank sheet of letterhead from an English manor house in which I stayed for a single night a decade ago. (*The Red House, Near Edenbridge, Kent*, it says grandly.) A sheaf of floor plans of my own apartment, a smudgy, scribbled witness to the difficulties I've had trying to make a home for myself in a twelve-by-eighteen-foot urban studio. Swatches of fabrics from years of redecorations. Articles, clipped from newspapers and magazines, about children's rooms and writers' studies. A much revised but still unfinished list of who will get which of my apartment's contents when I die.

A box of houses, I realized suddenly when I sorted through it last week—a carton of rooms real and imaginary, verbal and visual, old and new. For years, I realized as I sifted through the untidy drifts of papers, I had unknowingly collected images, memories, stories, and facts about homes. I'd hoarded them the way a starving person might collect recipes, loved them as a fan might cherish photos of favorite stars—there was a sort of yearning in them that startled me, and a kind of obsession.

Looking at my carton full of houses, you might think I was homeless, or adrift, or wandering. You might guess that mine had been a life uprooted in infancy, displaced by war, unhoused by disaster or poverty or fire. But it wasn't like that at all. My childhood was anchored by a single big, welcoming house, my adulthood sheltered by one small but always secure apartment. Someone glimpsing my life from the outside might say that, if anything, it was too stable, too settled, too domestically fixed. No actual unhousing inspired my collection of homes. As I closed the carton, I began to wonder what it was that drew me so persistently to these images: what sense of loss, and what sense of longing.

Inside

Outside, the weather was cold and drably grey, but inside its columned entrance the Metropolitan Museum was filled with color, movement, warmth. The pockets of gloom inside—the hushed dimness of the Medieval Hall, the spot-light-pierced darkness of a Celtic gold exhibit—were deliberate and theatrical. The scale of things inside the museum awed me: the urns of apple blossoms taller than my father, the crowds in the Great Hall as populous as a small city, the domed ceiling hundreds of feet above. I felt almost sick with the importance of it all, from the sweet, rich odor of the flowers to the women's sharp faces and eager staccato talk.

It was 1965, and I was nine, on a rare outing alone with my father. My brother and sister had been left at home to do chores and play Go Fish with my mother; for once I had the pleasure and the responsibility of choosing a destination on my own. I had never been to the museum before, and I had no idea of what I would find there, but I knew somehow that it was an important place. It was that significance, not the art, that I wanted. I had dressed suitably for the splendor of the occasion, in my favorite pop-bead pearls and a hot-pink pin-striped minidress made of some spongy synthetic material. My thigh-high tights, made for fleshier legs than mine, needed constant tugging to stay up, and I wore hopelessly awful blue glasses dusted with iridescent sparkles. But in my own mind I was radiant. No bride, no religious postulant, no chrysalis could feel more ready for transformation than I did. It was the first time I remember feeling that sensation, that urgent, sudden readiness for change.

The museum was not, in those days, a very welcoming place, and my father and I trudged from one gallery to the next with more doggedness than actual pleasure. My feet hurt, and I was ashamed of my drooping tights. Transformation did not occur, though a Pollyanna voice inside me insisted that it waited along the next marble corridor, down the next set of stairs.

We were looking for something I can't remember—the Impressionist paintings, maybe, or maybe just the restroom—when we walked through an archway and happened upon what seemed like another place, time, and climate. There was a room there, set apart from the hallway by a red velvet rope. It was luxurious, subtle, glowing, still. Even to my unsophisticated eyes it was obviously a room from the past, but it hinted at human presence, as if its occupants had just by chance wandered casually away. The chair near the desk had been left slightly askew and a book lay open on its seat. What seemed to be the weakly golden sun of a misty afternoon slanted through the tall windows. The round white-draped table was fully set. There was a book on the small desk, a clock on the mantel, even a dusty wine bottle stuck in a wooden stand.

My father wandered across the hallway while I stood at the velvet rope. What I felt there wasn't admiration or interest or the reasoned appreciation I've felt looking at art a thousand times since. It was passion, pure and simple. I fell in love with the room's calm, its order, its silence, its perfect stillness. With its solitude and its sureness. With the way everything in it went together, making something so perfect that it was tinged with a kind of grief.

The rooms I knew were comforting, miscellaneous places.

My family's kitchen had a patched ceiling and a linoleum floor always smudged with foot or paw prints. The bedroom I shared with my younger sister was wrapped in Beatles wallpaper blurrily printed with pictures of the Fab Four, and carpeted in some matted beige stuff that held an old Silly Putty stain in the corner near one bed. Our rooms were earnest and communal. Our house was a compromise between what we could afford and what we wanted, between the inherited past and the limitations of the present, between the needs of one person and of the next. I could no more have extrapolated the Met's room from those dense and improvised spaces than I could have imagined the potent, distinctive taste of chèvre from eating orange American cheese. I fell in love with the difference between the Met's room and my life.

The Met's little room gave that trip to the museum all the significance I had craved. In the classical myths I was just learning, transformation was always an ambiguous gift, and this one was no exception. The Met's room linked the form of a house to the shape of a life, convincing me by its sheer perfection that both could be serene, solitary, unerring, totally assured. It took me a long time to realize that the Met's room was an illusion, a room moved far beyond what a real room could be: an archetype that represented not ordinary life at all, but rather art, or maybe just manipulation. In the end I had to try to unlearn the half-conscious expectations it gave me. Some symbols have too much significance; rather than inspiring dreams, they are dispiriting high-water marks, against which real experience always comes up short.

ROOM FROM BORDEAUX, FRANCE, C. 1785, the Met's label says. Carved and painted pine paneling. Tentatively attributed to Barthelemy Cabirol, woodcarver. Tentatively located to the Hotel Razin de Saint-Marc, still standing today in the Cours D'Albret in Bordeaux. Furnished in the neoclassical mode with pieces from the period, though not from the original room. Satinwood escritoire. Tulipwood chairs. Silver-gilt clock and chandelier.

The Bordeaux room seems spacious but is actually very small. High ceilinged and circular, it is roughly eighteen feet across. Its single, curving wall is pierced by pairs of doors, niches, windows, and mirrors. As in a clock or compass face, each element is balanced, across the room, by its twin. A window faces a pair of doors of the same size, a niche another niche; the mirror over the console table literally and figuratively reflects the mirror over the fireplace. It's a rhythmic space, quietly pulsing, full of doublings and repetition.

Like most eighteenth-century interiors, the Met's room has no single determinable function. It is furnished with a desk, several chairs, and a dining table, all designed in a delicate rectilinear style. Unusually for upper-class rooms of its period, though, this one is almost plain. The paneling is ungilded, carved in low relief with sober vignettes of Architecture, Poetry, Art, and, incongruously to modern sensibilities, Farming. The gentle dull green of the paneling, the soft rose and grey of the silk swags lining the windows, the ivory and rose of the upholstery, the mustards and blues of the small Beauvais carpet are all greyed colors—subtle, almost silvery. They give the room an insubstantial quality, a gently melancholic, even elegiac, air.

But for all its restraint, it's a luxurious space. Once you notice the glint of gold, you notice it everywhere: on the chair frames and porcelain dishes, the hardware of windows and doors, the chandelier and sconces, even the ornate gilt-bronze clock on the mantel, with its figure of Venus whipping her chariot on. The textures are rich, inviting: the dense, thick warmth of velvet, the fluidity of silk, the mellow gloss of satin- and fruitwood. Ultimately neither sensual delight nor self-discipline triumphs in this room. It's a place that subjects its own opulence to order, that honors both the senses and the mind.

Of course, the unity that I loved is an illusion. In fact, all of it is reconstructed, some of it from sources and makers that can no longer be traced. The color of the paneling is re-created from a shade discovered under the repaintings of decades, but whether it's actually the original hue is anyone's guess. The fireplace and floor are not original, and the painted panels themselves had to be dismantled, numbered, shipped, and painstakingly reassembled in New York, a continent away from home. It's no longer possible to tell for sure who commissioned or lived in the original room, how it was used, or even what its windows looked out onto before the Met rebuilt them only inches away from the dead end of a blank ivory wall.

I didn't understand in 1965 that the Bordeaux room isn't a room at all but an exhibit, constructed not in 1785 but in 1943, not for use but for education—that it's a simulation of everyday life intended not to house or please but to instruct. I didn't understand that it was a so-called period room, or know how complicated the enterprise of making and looking at such a thing could be.

Museum period rooms attempt to capture the essence of domestic rooms, but they inevitably ignore—overturn, really—the most essential qualities of "roomness." They fix a room's flux, its mutability, into a permanent moment, as a butterfly is impaled on a pin. They reconstitute a felt experience as a seen one, substituting vision for touch. They replace the particular taste of a person with the general taste of an era. They make a private domain into a public monument. Empty as it is of human movement, warmth, bulk, chatter, and scent, of shifting or flickering light, of mess or clutter— devoid, in fact, of anything that might obscure its precise and confident perfections—it's no wonder that the Bordeaux room seemed so impossibly beautiful to me, so superhumanly serene, so worthy of emulation.

Like modern biographers and historians, the best modern museum professionals recognize how inevitably recreations color the past with the present, imposing a spurious order on what was chaotic, or at least complex. A museum installation of three period chairs on a plinth refuses to overnarrate; it leaves open space around things. It's a reminder that however abundant their documentation, the objects of the past almost always come into our hands as flotsam and jetsam: torn away from their relationships and enclosures, buffeted and even transformed by the wreckage of time.

Still, installations like the Bordeaux room do something the exhibition of isolated objects can't: They make educated guesses about the relationships within rooms—about the collaborative, interactive, accumulative nature of interior spaces. They speak to the harmonies and discords of colors, the complexities of density and scale, the influence of light. However foreign or archaic they look, they affirm the daily life we all, in some way, share.

Because of this, good period rooms have a sort of heart. They are not just beautiful but lovable. This is why the Bordeaux room spoke so powerfully to me when I was nine, before I knew where or what France was, before I knew the difference between rococo and neoclassical, before I could have imagined caring about the history of domestic interiors or the proper placement of a desk along a wall. Even then I had seen enough rooms to know that this one was different, and to be fascinated and moved by that difference. I didn't get as far as real comprehension, much less accuracy. But the experience was enough to inspire years of further lookings and relookings, of searchings and research.

In 1975 I was a sophomore at Douglass College, a part of New Jersey's state university. I lived with my roommate, Betsy, in a small old clapboard house, part of a horseshoe of such houses built in the twenties for faculty and later converted into dorms. They were remote and outdated, but Betsy and I thought they suited our bohemian style better than the bland convenience of the other dorms. In our twelve-by-fourteen-foot second-floor room we had two single beds, two maple dressers, two desks, two desk chairs, a miniature refrigerator, and a nightstand. The walls were a nondescript yellow, the buckled linoleum floor a streaky brown. The room was comically cramped. Our beds were exactly eighteen inches apart. I couldn't get to my closet when Betsy was at her desk, and she couldn't open her dresser drawers without blocking the door. Both of us had to navigate with care, stepping around the tangle of extension cords that connected our refrigerator, hair dryers, typewriters, and desk lamps to the two small outlets located in fiendishly inconvenient places near the floor. Ostensibly the home of two newly independent grown-ups, it was actually not very different from the room I'd shared with my sister at home, and its lack of privacy offered an unacknowledged but welcome excuse for not sampling college's more unfamiliar sexual freedoms.

Our need to assert ourselves in the face of the drab impersonality of the room, the school, and the world was much more compelling than the common sense that urged a minimal approach to this cramped space. All the extravagance, the boldness, the excess I craved in my life expressed themselves in my room. Betsy and I used every surface, we covered every inch: with brick-and-board bookcases that we stacked on our dressers and desktops; with posters of the Unicorn Tapestries and Degas ballerinas on my side of the room, of Bob Dylan and Chartres cathedral on Betsy's; with racks for cocoa mugs and pizzeria menus; with calendars and postcards, snapshots and greeting cards, woven baskets and Indian embroideries. We hung posters from the cornices with string and metal clips, taped snapshots and postcards to the bottom of the posters, put lamps and a popcorn maker atop the plank shelves, and leaned the wobbly bookshelves themselves against the walls. Our room had the impermanent, ornamental feverishness of a Gypsy camp. I heard the term *horror vacui* for the first time that year, and recognized my room immediately. At the end of the year we rolled up the artwork, boxed the books, tossed the bricks out the window into the woods behind.

I often took the bus to New York and visited the Met's Bordeaux room, approaching it as reverently and obsessively as a pilgrim does Rome. I looked at it desperately, as though it could complete me, supply me with all the qualities that I lacked. If I waited until the corridor was quiet and narrowed my eyes, the velvet rope of the doorway, the didactic label on the wall, and the chips in the ivory wall behind the windows all blurred out of view. For a moment I could will myself into an existence where I was not visitor to but owner of that room. Where it was late afternoon on a foggy day, and I was alone in my own home, reading a novel or just musing by the fire, waiting to be joined by a few sophisticated dinner guests. Where I was never rushed or anxious. Where I never worried about the gaucheness of my conversation or the size of my breasts. The room seemed to exude sensuality, yet it seemed, also, infinitely removed from what I felt were the body's confusions. If I could inhabit such a calm and sensuous place, I half believed, all the sexual and social unsureness that afflicted me would fall magically away.

That year my sense of self had changed from week to week, even from hour to hour. But the Bordeaux room had, I thought, survived for two centuries. Even in its new home at the Met, it had endured unaltered, while I had changed beyond recognition. Its curves and balances, its unfading faded greys, its endlessly anticipated dinner, even its light— the elegiac glow from the windows, the tender illumination of the sconces and chandelier—all seemed to sing me a lullaby of stasis and endurance, of permanence and peace.

❧

By 1985 I lived in a small apartment only thirteen blocks from the Met. I had moved into the city a few years earlier, but I'd never gotten fully settled. I had abandoned my impractical dreams of museum work and taken a job on Wall Street. I wore navy pinstriped suits with little silk bow ties. I was in love—unhappily, dramatically, obsessively—with a charming but elusive man who was more an addiction than a companion. Unless he had other plans, I spent my time in his apartment, a place larger and more luxurious than anything I could aspire to myself. Nights at my own apartment seemed incomplete. I felt anxious, uncomfortable, very alone. In my much longed for apartment, I missed living in my family's busy cluttered house, but I wouldn't have dreamed of telling anyone so.

The silence of my apartment bothered me, and so did its smallness. It was a studio, about twelve by eighteen, with a separate kitchen, a bath, and a hallway. People said it was charming. To me it felt cramped and oddly changeable. How could the same apartment seem at once yawningly lonely and yet too small to entertain a single guest in comfort? Every arrangement of my furniture seemed to sacrifice something indispensable. If I had a dinner table, I didn't have room for a desk. If I kept the double bed—which felt so important to my image of myself—I didn't have room for a comfortable chair. I felt as though I would have to jettison whole parts of myself, whole needs and interests, to make my home and my life work.

Despite this, I could never quite abandon the hope that my single cramped room might somehow transform itself into an inviting, calm, sufficient world. I puttered and tinkered and moved things around, only to be confronted with the same uneasy compromises, the same hard choices. As I did, I understood for the first time how illusory the perfections of the Bordeaux room were, or at least how privileged: how much time, how much money, how much space, how much domestic help was needed even to approximate them. I sensed for the first time that the condition of my life was not going to be extravagance or limitlessness, that I would probably never have that much of anything, that maybe no one did. I began to feel how my own fluctuating emotions wove themselves into the texture of my home. I began to understand how little the Bordeaux room had to do with the way I would live my life and inhabit my houses.

But I still loved it. Full of nesting instinct and capable at best of achieving an uneasy truce with the place in which I lived, I needed a home to admire, to cherish, to covet. The Bordeaux room still gave me that. I visited the Met every few weeks. Standing before the Lucite panels that now replaced the red velvet ropes, I lingered over the room's lines and colors the way someone lonely might savor the imagined face of a movie star or a fantasy lover, unconcerned with probability or possession, content simply to believe that such perfection exists. The Bordeaux room, and period rooms in general, began to seem like the mixed-up memories I cherished of times I could never recapture: pleasurable, necessary, to be treasured not because they're the real thing but because they're what I have.

❧ ❧

Like love for human beings, love for a room is an instinctive thing, essentially unexplainable and elusive. I'm not sure why the Bordeaux room speaks to me so powerfully, as though it corresponds to something I've dreamed or imagined or, some would say, lived before. Many of my friends see in it just another example of outdated ornamentation: fussy, formal, irrelevant. Loss being the risk of love, maybe one day I'll come to agree. I might lose the feeling of rightness and fulfillment this room gives me. I might lose my ability to suspend myself in its illusion, to ignore the museum's barriers and the false electric glimmer of the candle flames, and begin for the first time to notice the chipping paint beyond the windows, where there once seemed to hang a radiant and irresolute fog.

❦

Over the years I've tried to photograph the Bordeaux room, impelled by a need to possess some tangible memento of this space that has been so important and so elusive. My first shots were taken with an Instamatic camera, stripped of its flashcube in deference to museum rules. Lit only by the artificial glow of window and candle bulbs, the pictures—vague images of windowpanes, latches, and draperies emerging from a dense, velvety gloom—were as beautiful as they were misleading. It was as though the room had reimagined itself as a brooding Caravaggio, all shadow erratically shot with brilliance, rather than the lucently poignant Chardin it really is.

Unsatisfied, I asked my brother to try again, with his more sophisticated camera. The combination of a long exposure and a handheld lens produced results just as inadequate as the first and just as beautiful, though in an entirely different way. This time the prints came out pale, blurred, and evanescent. The photographs look trembly and faded, as if they had been printed on the thready gossamer of old watered silk.

I've kept both sets of pictures, not as the tokens of psychic ownership I'd hoped for but as reminders of the foolishness of the project. It's come to seem interesting to me that images of this reconstruction misconstrue it as thoroughly as the reconstruction misconstrues the long-lost room it's based so loosely on. It seems right that this space that falsely fixes time is itself so difficult to fix.

❧ ❧

When I last visited the room I realized that what attracts me to it now is partly the way it achieves a hesitant, impossible balance between the extremes of human possibility. It's a monument both to the senses and to the mind, a formal, orderly space that can enclose an intimate informality. Its complexity of surface is restful, its simplicity deeply complex. It's a space that accommodates both sensuality and solitude, and that merges the male and female principles well enough to dismantle the false distinctions between the rational and the intuitive, the firm and the fluid, the precise and the suggestive. Small enough to make a comfortably close shelter for the private self, it's also large enough to welcome the other. It's a timeless product of a vividly idiosyncratic time, an accessible public expression of a very private vision. If I believed in heaven, I would imagine it as something like this, not any one particular quality but the intersection, the dialogue, the enduring marriage of qualities, a union in which

inside   27

each informs and enriches the other through gentle opposition.

Glancing past the barrier at its door on this visit, I noticed how obsessed with circles the room is, how prominent a role arcs and curves and spheres play in its harmony. Rectangles appear in doorways and fireplaces, chair frames and windows, but they serve in some sense to counter and intensify a world otherwise without corners, angles, ends.

Some of the circles—the flat disks of floor and ceiling, the face of the clock, the bowls of the dishes—are unbroken ones. Each point in their circumferences clasps the next; they are images of completion, enactments of continuity. More common in the room, in its mirror frames and chair arms, its draperies and its carpet, are imperfect circles: curves that have not yet reached fulfillment, semicircles still straining toward completion, arcs that have over- or under-reached. Like so much else in this room, these two kinds of forms balance and complement each other. The perfect circle is enlivened and humanized by the energy, the ambition of the sweeping, partial arc and curve; the gesture of the half circle is explained by the sphere it will never be.

Entrance Hall One

The road to my grandparents' house was marked with signs and icons. We drove down the Garden State Parkway past the neon beer bottle tilting tipsily above the Pabst factory in East Orange; past the billboard Dutch Boy who sat, placidly holding his paint can, above the sluggish Passaic River; past the huge wooden horse's head that welcomed us to Monmouth County, a sign that I felt marked our entrance into a realm of delights but actually advertised only the local racetrack. Fifteen minutes beyond it, in the old shore town of Deal, we reached my maternal grandparents' house at 35 Monmouth Drive. More complicated than bottle or boy or horse's head, it was no less magical, no less larger than life.

I wasn't quite sure what that house stood for, but I knew it stood for something. It had a kind of significance for me that my own house didn't have, partly because it was exotic and mysterious to me. I learned about adulthood from it, or so I thought, and the expectations it raised were no less powerful for being mostly wrong.

The house in which I grew up was not quite big enough to be spacious, not quite old enough to be quaint. My grandparents' house was what is usually called a mansion, though a modest one compared to its imposing neighbors. Built in 1900, it had three stories, a turret, a deep, shady porch and a sharply angled green roof. Its style was substantial and sober, its elegance expressed in good proportions and fine details rather than lacy excrescences. It stood, with its carriage house and a little child's playhouse, on an incongruously small lot, the back garden having been sold off by a former owner during the Depression.

The Atlantic was two blocks away—by my child's count, six houses. You couldn't see the ocean from the house, but clues to its presence were everywhere. The crashing sound of the waves and the pervasive smell of clean, salt dampness. The veiny, translucent ocher stones that lined the driveway and paved the beach jetties—a duplication that intrigued me. The crystal bowl of shells that sat on the hallway table. Even the annual visit of house painters, hired by my grandfather and usually tipsily unreliable, who came each spring to recoat the white shingle and green trim faded from the continuous buffeting of the wet shore wind.

Inside, there were seven bedrooms, two staircases, a conservatory, a butler's pantry, a sixty-foot living room with a fireplace at each end, and five bathrooms, each done with a different tile: pale green and lavender as gently opalescent as fish scales in my grandmother's bathroom, severe pale blue in my grandfather's, and in the powder room downstairs a flamboyant Italian majolica, cobalt blue and marigold yellow and persimmon orange.

But here already the contradictions of the house assert themselves. This description makes it sound ostentatious and imposing, a stately home. But it wasn't entirely that, not even to a child with eyes as impressed by glitter as by gold, in love with the elaborate, overawed by the scale of the adult world. The texture of life in that house was deliberate and plain. Its luxuries were cheerful beach towels carefully washed, rolled to starched flatness on a mangle, darned, and set out year after year; or plain vanilla ice cream, Breyers or Sealtest, portioned out as meticulously as caviar. Its sensualities were the joys of sitting in a deep, steaming tub, feeling the grit of beach sand wash down the gurgling drain, and then stepping, flushed and scoured, into soft clean cotton pajamas—of falling asleep under the warmth of a knobby candlewick bedspread to the endless, unresolved tumble of the ocean waves. The order, cleanliness, and continuity of the place were no less privileges than the formal staircase or the butler's pantry, but the two were different sorts of luxuries, born of different values.

Life in that house wasn't so much grand as it was marbled with grandeur, veined with it like granite flecked with ore. The house was contradictory, a mixture of things opposite but inextricable, like my grandparents' marriage itself. My grandparents never seemed to argue, but neither did they agree. Their house voiced their differences, expressing what was then forty and is now seventy years of assertion and resistance, apology and serenade. It was a mannerly argument, conducted in civilized tones. Neither ever won, and neither ever had the last word.

※ ※

My grandfather bought the house on Monmouth Drive in 1959, on impulse. Despite his haste, it was a good buy, cheap because it was big and hard to heat. Joe's native shrewdness worked despite his habitual hurry, and many of the things he bought—antiques, buildings, investments, cars—would have made him a profit if he hadn't sold them as precipitously as he had bought them, to chums rather than strangers, over tumblers of scotch in bars, for less than the going price.

My grandfather was a gambler and a drinker, an entrepreneur, an extravagant, a man self-confident and often self-absorbed. Well into his nineties he bought quickly and what he calls "the best." Not for him the research of the true shopper, the minute deliberations, the haggling over price. He's a man who likes to buy expensive things quickly, who even likes to overpay—likes the rapidity and dash of it, the hint of daring and recklessness. The first of his family to break out of immigrant insecurity, he hates stinginess, smallness, and uncertainty. He has always bragged about expenses carelessly shouldered, bets lost, and money given away, but never about money saved or bargains struck. He has always welcomed danger, but can never stomach caution.

The oldest and much spoiled son of an Irish engineer, he came back from the France of 1918 to lead a rambunctious, itinerant existence as a prizefighter and oil wildcatter, a traveler on tramp steamers, a speculator who made money fast and lost it just as quickly. He settled down only after he fell in love with my grandmother, the shy, plain daughter of a Newark carpenter. At first she didn't want to marry such an unpredictable man, but eventually they both surrendered: she to a life more exciting and uncertain than she'd dreamed, he to the sedate business of running an insurance company. He remained a great gambler on the horses and a heavy drinker. He didn't give up the hearty male pleasures of racetracks, golf courses, and taverns until illness and age forced him into sedateness, and he was well into his seventies by then.

Though he was a complicated, bewildering husband and an unpredictable father, to the eyes of a young grandchild he was an adventure story come to life. We children took his boasts at face value, unconscious of the worry in his wife's face when he gambled or the tension in his daughter's when he drank. We loved his handmade Stetsons and his Havana cigars with their ornate paper rings, his tall tales and his jokes, his generosity and his laughter. We were beguiled by his air of bravado and even by the air of faint female disapproval that always attended him, whether he was urging us to race around the house until we were dizzy or taking us on trips to what he told us was Mexico (really the Norwood Inn's dark-paneled bar, where he would buy us Shirley Temples and drink for hours with his pals).

As though my grandmother's thrift taunted him, he brought her his bountiful plunder: a black velvet opera cloak and a set of apple green jade jewelry, Irish lace tablecloths and Caruso recordings. The Monmouth Drive house gave him a project large enough to accommodate his energies. At auctions, at junk shops, at sales of all kinds, he would find a sixty-foot Turkish carpet, a baby grand piano going cheap, a vast Turneresque oil of a ship at sea, a group of Victorian hunting bronzes, grisly sculptures entitled *The Stag at Bay* or *The Death of the Fox* (which I hated), a group of Dresden figurines (which I loved). Some of what he brought home was junk. I remember a cardboard box filled with silk drapery tassels and another crammed with the glittery, useless danglers from some long-dismantled chandelier. But some of his purchases were genuinely good: English china and American brilliant-cut glass, an elegant ivory Kwan Yin, and a small eighteenth-century bronze Diana, naked and holding a tightly strung bow.

My grandmother was as cautious as her husband was profligate. His impulsive gestures were foreign to her deliberate, steady pace. Still, she had been schooled in compliance by a traditional German father, six brothers, and Joe himself, and she accepted his purchases without argument. Later she would tell me, with a rare note of irony, that antiques, however haphazardly bought, were sounder investments than cases of bourbon or bets on the four-thirty at Belmont.

Once in her hands, even the most exotic objects seemed to root themselves, to find a stable meaning and a proper place, like the geranium cuttings she clipped from her plants, pushed into pots of clean peat and left, watered but untouched, until they had sent down sturdy filaments into the soil. She found a dark spot for the morbid bronzes, set the porcelains symmetrically in cabinets, hung the heavy paintings, domesticated a huge Satsuma vase by filling it with flowers from her own garden: red emperor tulips in the spring, Peace roses in summer, and in the fall, the silvery disks of something she told me was called either honesty or the money plant. All these bright objects seemed domesticated by her care, like tigers tamed into house pets.

One of my grandfather's finds was Indian, a cylindrical pagoda with a tiny brass man standing on its concave top. The little figure, an inch or so high, stood rigidly with his hands at his sides, holding in each fist a curved arc of brass wire that ended in a small spherical weight. When my grandmother put it on a low shelf so that we children could play with it, she told us that the little temple was an incense burner and that the brass figure was a demonstration of "equilibrium." I puzzled over the odd, unfamiliar word. Spun fast or slowly, pushed or poked, he wouldn't fall, so well balanced was he by his equal pendant weights. Instead, he'd spin, dizzy but upright, whirling quickly around the imperceptibly curved bowl of his pagoda until inertia finally slowed him and he stood motionless again.

I loved the coldness of the brass, even on sweltering days, the sense of mastery I got from knowing the exact motion— a quick, neat twist—that would send him turning at maximum speed. But my grandmother's promise of equilibrium was false. He spun and balanced only on his own terms, on his own small platform with its carefully shaped and circumscribed boundaries. Too violent a flick of the wrist, too strong a punch from a finger, and he skittered helplessly off his pagoda. Once beyond it, he was awkward and useless, his balance gone. He couldn't stand upright, since his weights hung down below his feet; he could only lie stiff and immobile on his back, like a soldier felled at war or a fish gasping on a dry sand beach.

❧ ❧

My grandmother was baptized Marie but always called Mitzi, a diminutive perfect for her small size and her unpretentious character. Her temperament is as stereotypically German—provident, industrious, stoic—as Joe's is Irish. Now in her nineties, she's survived broken hips, stomach cancer, and in recent years, the deaths of two of her four children. Endurance like hers didn't mean much to me as a child. What I admired then was her crisp elocution—her favorite word was "properly," and she pronounced it ringingly, with full emphasis on the second *p*—her immaculate grooming, her knowledge of antiques, and her membership in the evocatively named Polar Bear Club, whose initiates swam in the Atlantic even in the winter.

By the time I knew her, her hair was almost completely white, but in girlhood it had been a red as fiery as the temper she habitually suppressed. Her skin, back then when she swam and gardened daily, was so thickly freckled that it looked tanned. Her voice was musical but subtly tinny, like a good piano gone slightly flat, the result of a botched sinus operation that had also taken away her senses of smell and taste. She never mentioned this to her grandchildren, instead accepting our gifts of cheap lavender toilet water with gratitude and squeezing the fruit for lemonade as carefully as if she could taste the result.

Mitzi rather guiltily enjoyed the diamond earrings and mink hats, the sterling flatware and Limoges china my grandfather gave her, but she didn't buy luxuries for herself. A child of a struggling family of seven and a young adult in the Depression, she still believed in making do long after the need to scrimp was past. She canned her own fruit, grew her flowers from cuttings or seeds, sewed her own children's clothes. She can be as intemperate in her prudence as my grandfather in his lack of it. To this day, my usually equable mother resents the dowdy homemade dresses that plagued her adolescence, products of her mother's unremitting thrift.

I associate Mitzi with her kitchen, a big, light, high-ceilinged space at the back of the Monmouth Drive house. It had a brick-patterned linoleum floor, walls clad halfway up with cream-colored tile, a plump old Westinghouse refrigerator, and a pitted porcelain sink with spindly legs. It was an old-fashioned room, filled with a reassuring hominess. My grandfather bustled through it on his way to the cellar, where he kept enough liquor to stock a speakeasy; to the driveway, where he kept the Lincolns he bought new each year; to the butler's pantry, where his spirits and mixers, martini glasses, and blown-glass swizzle sticks were stored. But in the kitchen itself, his magpie habits left no mark, and his impetuosity made no impression.

The rest of the house was solidly Victorian, but the kitchen reprised the thirties and forties, a world recognizable but not quite modern. The kitchen table with its yellow wooden legs and its red oilcloth cover; the glazed tinware ladles and colanders, mustard brown with narrow green rims; the checked curtains with their border of cheerful nodding farmers; the cream jug in the shape of a cow and the Franciscan earthenware with its pattern of bamboo shoots and branches: my grandmother's kitchen possessions suited that comfortable, dated room as perfectly as if they had been bought with it.

They hadn't, of course. Mitzi had packed and moved them many times, to the row houses in Newark and Belleville, where my mother grew up; the Maryland farm, where they spent the war years; the apartment in Bloomfield, from which the Deal house was bought. Once she grew used to something, my grandmother never gave it up, whether it was a Haviland tureen or a plastic dish-detergent squeeze bottle that fit her small hand. Each time she moved she would swaddle her things in stiff folds of newsprint, nest them lovingly in Chivas or Johnny Walker cartons, label each box with her lapidary script, then reverse the whole process at the other end. I think this laborious ritual of protection and restoration was her reminder of the continuity of her life, her assertion of safety and control. It helped make all her kitchens places of luminous timelessness. The Deal kitchen was a world that fit together: brushes with their dustpans, saucepans with their lids, farmers bowing in eternal amity, the china cow reunited with her clean white milk, all fitting as perfectly within their enclosure as snails within their shells.

In the gloomy dining room, my grandmother used crystal saltcellars with tiny silver spoons, but in the kitchen she had a chromium stand with a spring contraption that held the small, bluntly faceted salt and pepper containers, with their red Bakelite tops, above the table surface. This was my favorite of her things. I liked the slight tug I had to give to release one of the shakers and the way the holder suspended them safely aloft, like a plump couple riding the boardwalk Ferris wheel. I loved the enduring, complementary marriage of the modest, sensible salt to the tempestuous pepper. Like the beach after high tide, most of the Monmouth Drive house sparkled with flotsam and jetsam, with oddities gleaming and random. The kitchen was a less complex, more reassuring place. Instead of the beauty of surprise, it had the beauty of inevitability, an air of things come home.

*   *

My grandfather sold the Deal house abruptly in 1967, when one of his real estate investments was in trouble and he needed the cash. My grandmother protested, but in the end she packed her boxes yet again. They moved to a smaller house, and then a still smaller one, until they finally came to rest in the 1960s Florida ranch house where they live today, surrounded by odds and ends of their solid Victorian furniture, which looks darkly bulky in the small, bright space. The bronze dying stag was left with the Deal house, the Dresden and the Diana sold quickly and cheaply, but my grandmother still keeps her cut glass in the safety of the same rosewood breakfront, taking a piece out now and then and turning it in the sunlight until the colors flash on the walls in brilliant disarray. The salt-and-pepper set was lost at some point, but the brass man survived all of his moves. Tarnished and dusty, he sits on the ledge of a bookcase in front of the books that are now too heavy for either of my grandparents to hold.

I was twelve when the Monmouth Drive house was sold. Deal is only fifty miles from my longtime home in Manhattan, but I've never been back. I toy with the idea of visiting it, sometimes, but in the end I never actually go, unwilling or maybe unable to see the house diminished by scattered tricycles on a badly seeded lawn, or demolished in favor of a condominium development.

Sometimes I wonder what it would have been like to come to that house filled with an adolescent's anarchic belligerence. I suspect that at fourteen or sixteen, hiding shyness under a love of loud songs and counterculture slogans, I would have been ambivalent about my grandparents' home. If there was a single thing that united Joe and Mitzi, it was, oddly, a belief in boundaries, in categories. Joe's were the clear-cut differences between heroic Americans and evil Japs, good and bad whisky, rich people and poor. Mitzi's were the subtler but no less rigid distinctions between the right word and the wrong one, the oyster plate and the fish platter, the man and the woman. They might not agree on the details, but both were equally comfortable within a world of hierarchies. Theirs was a home in which the ideas of male and female, stranger and family, adult and child were as enduring and distinct as the classical orders, and they both took for granted that only by giving each its separate due could harmony be assured.

But at twelve—a shy, bookish, backward twelve—I still

felt comforted by my grandparents' habits and certainties. I felt somehow reassured by the separations in their house: between the kitchen china and the formal china, the drawer of tattered books for children and the far more fascinating, grown-up volumes that stood safely behind glass. I loved the contrast between the back door—a plain metal storm-screen affair to which milk and groceries were delivered—and the formal front entrance, a salvia-bordered walk that led to a glossy white door with a leaded fanlight. I loved the fact that the back staircase, which we children used on our forays to the beach, was narrow and steep, its steps covered with sharply ridged black rubber treads, while the wide stairs of the front entrance had rose-colored carpet and ma-hogany balusters. They rippled graciously upward, stopping in midflight to pool in a wide landing before rushing on again in a generous swoop, and they were reserved for adults or—with permission—for children impeccably clean and well be-haved.

These separations sound oppressive to me now. Back then they reassured me, filled me with an abiding image of adult-hood as a distinct and privileged thing. From the vantage point of my childhood's plain everyday life, it seemed to be a world as crisp as my grandmother's ironed towels, as elegant as the majolica bathroom, as brilliant as her intricately cut glass. I assisted at its rituals like an acolyte patiently serving the dimly comprehended mysteries of the altar. Helping my grandmother set the dining room table with its translucent plates and damask tablecloth made me look forward to the day when I would take my place—assured, sophisticated, graceful—amid its sugar tongs and saltcellars. Scraping my bare feet on the back stairs' rough treads made me anticipate the day when I would be married on the landing of the front stairs, as my grandfather always promised I would be.

Happily, I didn't see these expectations as the ambiguous gifts they were: didn't recognize that they were as doubled as a clamshell, didn't know that they were at once beautiful dreams and guarantees of loss. I didn't realize that my grandfather would sell the house long before I could be married in it, or that the precisely ordered rituals my grandmother cherished had long been things of the past. It didn't occur to me that the delicate and opulent things I learned to love in that house might turn out to be cumbersome possessions, or that when I finally got to adulthood I'd find not a realm of distinct powers but something as muddied and unresolved as the ocean waves. I grew up expecting a grown-up life as confidently clear-cut as that house. I was surprised and a little disconcerted when I arrived in a world where adults felt impatient with formality, distrustful of distinctions, and nostalgic for the free, uncomplicated vision of the child.

Playroom

Now that I'm grown up I think of play as something
carefree and undirected, but when I was a child I played
urgently, as though something was at stake. The toys that

preoccupied me most were miniature houses of various sorts, and I made, deconstructed, and decorated them with the fierce persistence of a scientist seeking a miracle cure. The malady that needed healing was a kind of crowdedness. If you'd asked me to diagnose myself, and if I had trusted you enough to tell the truth, I would have told you I suffered from a surfeit of fellow children.

Our New Jersey neighborhood was lined with big, shabby houses, whose six or nine or ten bedrooms attracted large families. The Learys from next door had twelve kids, the Bateses down the block nine, the Trevors six. The driveways and backyards of our block were silent only late at night, on schooldays, and on Sunday mornings, when everyone but the aged, the infirm, and my family went to Mass. The grassy lots that divided the block from the town's main street were veined with tracks worn to bare, packed dirt by children trudging to Fiegelson's candy store and back, and even the small woods at the north end of Arlington Avenue, the wildest locale most of us could imagine, were dense with tree houses, log forts, and the cryptic painted markers of the neighborhood's secret clubs.

By local standards my family's three children seemed pitifully few. To me they seemed ample, maybe excessive. My younger sister was one of those ebullient kids who draw attention as magnets attract iron filings; I felt insignificant in the face of her charm and energy. My brother was my twin. From before I could remember, he had inhabited my life with me, sharing everything from punishments to bedtime stories, suffering the same hurts and fears, fighting for the same approval. When we were toddlers, his presence was as necessary and normal to me as my own. It required no thought, no conscious accommodation. But by the time I was five or so, his constant presence was bittersweet to me, at once deeply beloved and subtly burdensome.

I loved my sister and brother, but I wished that they were, not exactly dead, maybe, but gone. I said nothing about this to anyone, barely admitted it to myself. I felt furtive and jittery with the power of my longing, like a timid terrorist carrying a detonator under her coat.

I learned to read early, loving the solitude of it, and read compulsively. I was happily unaware of how many of my favorite stories—Frances Hodgson Burnett's *Secret Garden* and *Little Princess*, Rumer Godden's *The Doll's House* and *Miss Happiness and Miss Flower*, and my favorite of favorites, encountered first in a *Reader's Digest* condensed version, *Jane Eyre*—were of solitary beings, loners, and misfits who sought a place rightfully their own. When I wasn't reading, I made small houses. They varied in size, shape, and purpose, but all of them had a single thing in common: they were places without children. Even in play I did not want to be surrounded by more infants, toddlers, playmates, siblings— by more rivals. I wanted a place where I could be in control, unique, and free to be alone.

I got my first toy house for Christmas the year I was six. It was a set of neat bricks that worked on the same interlocking principle as today's Lego toys. The plastic bricks were all the same size, and they came in only three variations: opaque white blocks for walls, clear ones for windows, and brownish red blocks, more or less the color of dried blood, that served for everything else. The only houses that could be built from them were sharp, neat, and of an almost surgical sterility. No signs of life, no real variation, no eccentricity was possible. It was as though the manufacturers imagined children as a race content to do nothing more than re-create the cookie-cutter homes and prefab gas stations so beloved in the tidy, anxious fifties.

I loved these cold inhuman blocks with a geometer's passion for abstract form. It was because they were so small, so simple, and so similar that they seemed to me miraculous. They reduced the complex universe that was a house into its most basic units; they moved it from the realm of the senses into pure and basic structure. They suggested that the diverse, shifting world was a unity, and one assembled from manageable little segments. They gave me my first conscious taste of the power of the creator, the artist, the god. Every time I held in my hand a brick's glassy unbreakable perfection or heard the pleasurable *click*, less sound than sensation, as its convex cap snapped neatly into the hollow base of another, I felt the satisfaction of creating something sturdily sound, immutably *right*. Every time I pulled one of those cold houses apart, sweeping the tidy rubble into its box, I savored the joy of control.

Eventually I lost interest in these abstract spaces and spent a few years playing, unsatisfied, with doll rooms made of molded plastic furniture arranged in shoeboxes. My dissatisfaction ended when I got my first Barbie doll, on my ninth birthday. My particular Barbie had a platinum blond bubble cut, impenetrable and oily; a small, bee-stung mouth colored a fashionable frosty pink; and permanent blue liner on her slanted eyes, whose molded wedges of black lash gave her a sullen, provocative look. Her body was the peculiarly emphatic shape standard in Barbie dolls of the early sixties, with high conical breasts, narrow waist and hips, long legs with pronounced calves, and tiny feet permanently arched for high heels. Today's Barbies, though they seem gimcrack and flimsy compared to their more solid predecessors, have a reassuring girlishness, a big-eyed and cheerful naiveté. The earlier doll was inscrutably, mysteriously sexual, pure woman, with no girlishness at all.

I dressed and re-dressed Barbie and her friends Ken, Midge, and Skipper endlessly, charmed by the cunning completeness of their ensembles the tiny matching shoes and purses, the minuscule necklaces and gloves, the gardening outfits that came with watering cans and trowels. I organized the clothing in the dolls' plastic carrying cases until it was as tidy as an operating theater. The only thing I didn't do, in fact, was actually play with the dolls. I admired Barbie, who reminded me of the full-blown, glamorously female beauty of my mother, but not for a moment did I believe that the adventures promised by her pouty lips or pneumatic breasts would ever be mine. I was a pragmatic, even pessimistic, kid; my imaginings of the future were already hedged and limited, shaped forever by my fall from blond and gorgeous infancy into an anomalous and awkward childhood of glasses, missing teeth, and an awkward, skinny frame. I felt unfit to share the fantasies Barbie embodied. She seemed equally unfit to share my dreams, in which I was either a princess ruling over a vast and lonely castle or Annie Oakley riding alone on the endless empty range.

But the idea of making a small house for Barbie captured my imagination in a way Barbie herself didn't. The first homes I made her were assemblages of found objects arranged inside walls made from the right angles of opened books. For kitchens and bedrooms I used *Reader's Digest* condensed books, which were covered with appropriately small-scaled and homey Colonial prints; for other rooms, the intensely colored endpapers of volumes of the *Golden Book Encyclopedia*. Each was a different, opulently beautiful shade; emerald and violet, sapphire and ruby, marigold and pumpkin, they made enclosures colorful enough for a Gypsy and regal enough for a queen. I scoured our house for furnishings and collected kitchen matchboxes for end tables, washcloths or scarves for rugs, jewelry cases for dressers, a tiny china piano that had come with a porcelain figurine, pieces from Clue and Monopoly as irons or candlesticks.

Barbie slept, splendidly exotic, in a slatted Japanese pencil case made up with handkerchief bedding, and dined on coat-button plates at a table that I made, unwittingly mimicking the manner of Charles and Ray Eames, of laboriously glued together layers of balsa wood. Nothing in these rooms matched in color, mood, or scale. I noticed their shortcomings but had no way of rectifying them until, one Christmas, I got something called Barbie's Dream House. The Dream House was a small cardboard suitcase that opened out to form the interior of an apartment. It came with sheets of printed and die-cut cardboard that folded and slotted themselves into Barbie's furniture. The Dream House and its contents were bright and boxy, in the modernistic style of the early sixties: bookshelves with solid blocks of books, a double bed with pillows as hard and round as cough drops, a breakfast bar, a wardrobe with a real rod for Barbie's hangers, even a console television on which stood a large rectilinear lamp and a stand-up picture of Ken.

The Dream House reflected an idea of home more sterile and less creative than my ad hoc assemblages. In that sense it was a step backward, a kind of shrinking from an idiosyncratic and anarchic vision of existence to a confined and stereotypical one. I didn't notice this, and I wouldn't have cared. This was my first dollhouse to have the consistent scale of a real home and the first to do justice to all the small, fascinating details of domesticity: the lamps and books, the rugs and dishes, the door and cabinet handles, the pictures and pillows. Because the furnishings had been made as a set, they were interlocking, interchangeable. I spent hours shifting them around, thrilled by how variously they could be fit into the same neat and orderly space.

The fantasies I enacted with this dollhouse ignored Barbie's sexual promise and the glamorous bachelorette existence the Dream House was intended to suggest. I fantasized not of merging but separation, yearned not for rapture but for clarity. The glimpses I'd gotten of intimacy and passion—the heated arguments of my ordinarily placid parents, the glimpse of our baby-sitter being awkwardly kissed by the college kid from next door, the rough teasing from a boy I thought was cute—still seemed like embarrassments to be avoided at all costs.

But the pleasures of having one's own space I already understood. Sharing a room with my sister and squabbling with my brother over toys, I had learned enough about closeness to want a place of my own. Punished for spilling ink on my rug or sent too early to bed, I appreciated the delights that might come from living alone, independent, accountable to no one. The compromises, crowdings, and disenfranchisements of childhood had already made me envious of adult autonomy and control.

I too, like Barbie, could one day be a single woman with a room of my own, free of sibling clutter and parental rule. I too would someday come home to the silence of my own apartment. I would line my tall, color-coordinated kitchen stools up perfectly under the edge of the breakfast bar and arrange my own knickknacks on my own shelves. I would pull my armchair and its matching ottoman out to welcome company or leave it close to my bookshelf for a night of peaceful reading. I did not dream of Barbie or myself going to parties, driving in a fancy car, getting married in a long white gown. I imagined each of us sitting at home alone, dependent on no one, solitary ruler of all she surveyed.

I grew out of Barbie, and at some point my mother or I threw or gave the Dream House away. By the time I was thirteen or so, I had moved on to a Victorian wooden dollhouse. My belated desire to have this kind of toy was a dreamy, befuddled mixture—of admiration for the safe, foggy, rigidly ordered nineteenth-century world I read about in Sherlock Holmes stories, *Jane Eyre*, and *Little Women*; nostalgia for my grandparents' beautiful Victorian house, which had been sold the year before; and pessimism about an adolescence that already, at this early date, promised to be a very bumpy ride.

The dollhouse was a simple wooden box about two feet square, with a sharply angled roof covered with round brown tiles. My father, who built it for me, liked things to be solid and foursquare, and made the shell of the house of incongruously thick, half-inch plywood; had it been full-scale, its walls would have been six feet thick. Inside, though, the proportions held true. The minuscule blown-glass port decanter was perfectly sized for the mahogany sideboard, the bead-and-wire chandelier scaled just right for the tiny Boucher print it pretended to light. Under the angles of the eaves I made a nursery lined with blue ticking-stripe paper; below, there was a bathroom with tiny porcelain fixtures, a bedroom, a somber dining room with gloomy mahogany furniture, and a crowded little parlor. I painted the outside with textured grey paint meant to look like stone, but the illusion didn't really work. I could envision the way I wanted the windows to look—tall, narrow casements with tiny square panes—but the balsa wood frames I made fell apart, and by the time I could afford the miniature windows in the doll-house shop, I'd moved on to other projects.

I spent hours decorating the house, delighted by my power to create a precise, orderly world in one-inch-to-one-foot scale. The humiliations of early adolescence were mag-ically held in a sort of quarantine during those hours, set apart, made harmless. So were my loneliness, my envy of my still-charming younger sister, even my pervasive self-consciousness. Charm didn't matter then, or social skills, or prettiness, or the just-right clothes and cool attitude that real-life seventh grade demanded; only care, precision, dex-terousness, and a dogged persistence.

My approach to earlier dollhouse efforts had been cava-lier. This time I aimed for exactitude and refinement. I re-searched Victorian design; bought stamps whose small engraved prints would serve, framed and varnished, as paintings; made chandeliers and wall sconces from twists of fine brass wire and tiny gold beads. I hung special dollhouse wallpaper, searched out dried flowers delicate enough for bouquets, sewed minute pillows for the beds, even scrib-bled a few tiny squares of paper with minuscule script for the rolltop desk. Slowly, through birthday and Christmas gifts and purchases made with carefully saved housecelan-ing money, I acquired a few pieces of good dollhouse furniture: an ornate brass bedstead, a glass-paned breakfront, a scrolled rocker upholstered in somber red plush. I even received a small doll family with nicely detailed porcelain heads. Rather guiltily, I tossed them into the box of dollhouse supplies I kept in my closet. There, for the entire time that the dollhouse sat in my room, they stayed, a carelessly abandoned family with bare, limp, muslin limbs.

My Victorian dollhouse was a rearguard action—a retreat as much as an advance. Barbie's house had been the easy, informal fantasy home of someone more or less like me, living, in some more or less recognizable future, a more or less independent life. The wooden dollhouse was a traditional family home rather than a single woman's pad, a place antiquated rather than progressive in design. It was a fantasy, not, as Barbie's house had been, of independence and solitude, but of solid, reassuring, timeless order. It reflected my fascination with another time and culture but also marked my discomfort with my own. A toy home steeped in nostalgia, it enacted the conviction of my thirteen-year-old self that security could be found only far away and long ago.

But despite its regressiveness, the dollhouse helped bring me forward into adulthood. For the first time I got the rest of the family involved in the process of my creation. Just as I'd asked for my father's help with the shell, I got my brother to lend a hand with the roof and went on furniture-buying forays with my mother and sister. My sister made a small dollhouse too, and—for once the more capable one—I helped her hang its wallpaper and arrange its rooms.

Built into my Victorian dollhouse, in fact, were the beginnings of its own abandonment. When I stopped work on it, wrapping its furniture and sticking it in a corner in our basement, I moved on to my own first apartment, an actual real-life home. I live in that same apartment today, and the dollhouse sits—cleaned and dusted after years of storage—in the corner. I no longer work on it; when I have time for puttering with houses, I work on full-scale curtains, stain real floors, hang life-sized prints. In one sense, though, I haven't changed much since I made it and all of those other dollhouses. At only three hundred square feet, my apartment is small enough to seem almost miniature, and I live here entirely alone.

Kitchen

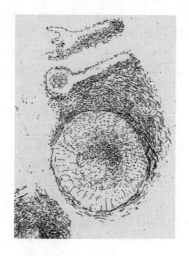

From the outside the junk drawer was unremarkable—

ordinary, shiny, syrup-colored maple faintly smudged with

fingerprints—but inside it was completely different from

the rest of my family's kitchen. The other drawers, cabinets, and cupboards held recognizable categories of things arranged in regular patterns: stacks of pot holders, rows of cookbooks and spices, nests of bowls, bins of cutlery. The junk drawer was unabashedly indiscriminate and unpredictable. It was crammed with pens, pencils, pink rubber erasers, a magnifying glass in a leather cover, an Esso key chain hung with four mysterious keys, three wishbones no one had ever wished on, two of the tiny parasols given out by the local Chinese restaurant, and a scattering of flower-shaped pink-plastic birthday-candle holders that smelled like sugar icing. The other drawers, cabinets, and shelves reached toward an idealized orderliness, a kind of purity that was based on exclusion: *no, that does not belong here.* In contrast, the junk drawer was as cheerful and forgiving as the foster families always being written up in the magazines my mother read, the kind that welcomed orphans too odd, impaired, or miscellaneous to find a home anywhere else.

Our entire kitchen was my mother's domain (I took this for granted: this was suburban New Jersey in the 1960s, and if there were kitchens where men ruled or even really labored, I never saw them), but the junk drawer seemed especially hers. Like her it relished the abundance of the world, embraced the flux and multiplicity of things. It had her common sense and her willingness to accept a less than perfect order. My mother kept her house tidy and her kids clean, but she did not worry about minutiae, about the unidentifiable foil-wrapped lumps that gradually accumulated in her freezer or the dust balls that danced deep under the sofa's skirts.

This worried my father, who is a precise and obsessively methodical man. My mother's blithe unconcern for petty neatness made him anxious and sometimes angry. Every few months or so some lapse of hers or his children's would drive him to fury. "Look at this mess!" he would yell, stabbing his finger at the clutter in the hall closet or a pile of clothes on one of our bedroom floors. "Why can't things be put where they belong? That's all I'm asking, damn it! Put things where they belong!" It was a passionate, futile cry. As a teenager I began to understand his frustration, but for most of my childhood my mother's relaxed housekeeping didn't trouble me at all.

Back then my mother seemed tall, though she's really of average height, five feet five or so. She has long legs and a full high bosom and an expressive, sharply angled face. In photographs from this time she looks vibrantly pretty, though an objective scrutiny might show lips a little too thin and bones a little too sharp for classic ideas of beauty. Her hair had begun to grey by the time I was born, and she dyed it at home with Clairol ash blond hair coloring, a metallic purple-brown gel with an acrid, almost industrial smell. She used wavy metal bobby pins, Maybelline eyebrow pencil, and rosy pink Coty lipstick, whose golden tube had a tiny pop-up mirror on top. She liked polka dots, and the color red, and high heels, which emphasized the narrowness of her already high-arched feet. On the rare evenings she and my father went out, she wore costume jewelry—little rhinestone clip-on earrings, a brooch in the shape of a leaf—and dresses culled from the clearance racks at Bambergers, S. Klein, and Ohrbach's. She wore her marked-down finery insouciantly, as though price and status were irrelevant, as though elegance could be conjured up from sheer self-confidence. On her way out the door, she would bend down and press her puckered, just-lipsticked mouth briefly against mine. I didn't like the sweet soapy taste, but I loved being imprinted with the mark of her femininity, the shadow of her glamour. I always wore the fading lipstick proudly until bedtime, like a badge of honor.

My father was the house's guardian. He mastered the practical workings of things, assigned the tasks, set the schedules. He was both the double-checker of details and the creative force behind all of our home-improvement projects. My mother's contribution to the house was more ephemeral. She was its muse, its anima, the goddess of its festivals and its harvests. She was less handy and less patient than my father when it came to domestic projects. Unlike him, though, she had in abundance the ability to accept things as they were and a love of the adventure of making much out of nothing—necessary, even redemptive, gifts.

She made elaborate productions out of inexpensive home-made birthday cakes, put together bright, inexpensive curtains, and painted cast-off furniture for our rooms. Out of the ordinary routines of a family home she created ceremonies and traditions. Sick days always meant toast cut on the diagonal and the chance to clean out her jewelry drawer, with its jumble of fake pearl necklaces, earrings with screw-on backs, and the tiny turquoise blue bracelets given to each of us as newborns. The Miss America Pageant (I admit this with some shame) was my special evening, and she would let me stay up late, serving me ginger ale in a wineglass and green grapes in a pink bowl, the most elegant and feminine treat I could think of. There was an air of splendor about these occasions, created mostly from her own unself-conscious enjoyment of them. She expected her children to be diligent about what she called "helping around the house," but she was never loath to abandon an afternoon of house-cleaning for trips to the grocery store, the park, the town sweetshop, or, later, the mall. She ferried us back and forth in decrepit, dented sedans—shark-finned relics from the fifties that she and my father, unable to afford a second new car, bought for $50 or $100 at local junkyards—with as much panache as if they were Bentleys, giving them elaborate names and making our mostly unsuccessful trips to car in-spection seem like epic quests.

I was twelve or thirteen when my delight in her impro-visatory splendor began to fade. I had by then learned just enough—about the world and about myself—to lose faith in this kind of magic. I had grown even more skinny, and gotten even thicker glasses, and seen Nancy Palmer get thirty valentines to my ten. I had spent afternoons in my friend Peggy's room, which had perfectly matched department-store French Provincial furniture and a white fur rug. It had become clear that a secondhand kiss of lipstick would not make me gorgeous, that a coat of paint was not enough to make cast-off dressers into Chippendales. Hoping for such transformations now seemed as foolish and risky as believing in Santa Claus.

But if I could not be glamorous or powerful or rich, I began to think, I could at least be acceptable, average, normal. If I could not be admired, I could at least be taken seriously. If I could not be charming, I could at least be capable, or educated, or refined. I became a teenage skeptic, and a teenage snob.

What had once enchanted me about my mother now seemed unbearably, even dangerously, eccentric. I still loved her and relied on her. But what I yearned for, not so secretly, was the bland, prim, upper-middle-class existence I glimpsed in her women's magazines. I dreamed of a house filled with matched Colonial furniture and color-coordinated throw pillows. Of a powder blue Princess phone in my own room, and lots of callers. Of a sedate, college-educated mother who played bridge, belonged to the country club, wore twin sets, and went to the market exactly once a week in a dignified Town and Country wagon.

I rebelled against my mother quietly, with the furtive resentment of the powerless. Instinctively I tried to outdo her in the only sphere where that seemed possible: the small workaday world of the house. Every task I undertook now proclaimed the inadequacy of her domestic habits and routines. Officiously I began to point out the grease-spattered disorder of the line of cookbooks near the stove and the cobwebs in the corner near the fish tank. I took on extra chores, pointedly reorganizing the china closet, cleaning out the medicine chest, sorting through the junk drawer with a visibly martyred air. When I vacuumed, I moved all the furniture, laboriously, as though merely swiping the nozzle under the dining room table would have been a moral fault. When I cleaned the bathroom I rubbed bleach-soaked cotton swabs along every grout line and, kneeling like a penitent, scoured under the faucets of the tub, where no one ever looked.

I felt a new allegiance with my father, whose frustration with my mother's slapdash housekeeping I could finally understand. Ironically, my sympathy for his thwarted tidiness didn't spare me from his wrath. Patrolling as cleanliness inspector in my mother's parts of the house left me little energy for my own room. It was littered with books, clothes, and half-finished art projects, always a terrible mess.

My mother took my defection from her fan club with grace. With the same equanimity that let her ignore her unalphabetized spice racks and messy stove-burner pans, she rose above my carping criticisms and my gratuitous assistance. Luckily for both of us, I decided it was time to get started earning my college money with a regular job. I went to register at the junior high student-employment office on a fall day the year I turned thirteen. Within a week I had been hired as a housecleaner—another fact whose irony I missed—for a family from the expensive new development north of town.

Barbara Robbins, my new employer, was tall and skinny, with a cropped cap of blond hair and a mobile, horsey face. She wore no-nonsense business suits, simple white tennis dresses, plain pearl earrings, and a man's gold wristwatch. She strode rather than walked, in an odd tiptoe, pigeon-toed gait that made her look as though she was always rushing forward. She did everything briskly, with no dawdling over inessentials, and she talked in a quick staccato patter. By the time we pulled up in her driveway that first day of work, she had told me about her husband, Ron, and her four sons, her crazy schedule, her job as a special education consultant to the school system, the symptoms of the autistic kids with whom she worked. I hadn't heard the term before, and I had trouble understanding why "artistic" children should be such a problem. I felt young, provincial, admiring. Even my inability to understand her impressed me, told me that she lived in a different world from mine, a place more affluent, more educated, more complex, to my eyes more acceptable. I was bewildered but awed, by her and, even more profoundly, by her house.

The Robbinses' house was vaguely French in style, with casement windows and a mansard roof. I could see that it was a pastiche, an elaborate suburban fake, but I forgave it for the glory of what was inside. There, I thought, things were real. The floors were not linoleum but flagstone, oak, walnut parquet, and in the kitchen, ruddy glazed brick. The formal living room had marquetry tables, a huge silver-gilt mirror, an astrolabe, and a pair of bay trees in square, ball-footed planters. The family room was crowded with a walnut partners desk, a zebra-skin rug, and a table designed specially for backgammon. In the Robbins house I saw netsuke, walk-in closets, bombé chests, and Jacuzzis for the first time. It was my introduction to a certain kind of high-bourgeois consumerism, the house of the women's magazines, the house of my dreams. It relied on no magic and required no compromises: the shell efficient and modern and in impeccable working order, the furnishings dramatic and eclectic, shining with assurance and expense.

It was Barbara Robbins's nature to streamline things, and she kept her house as impersonally as a hotelier. Her four sons' rooms were furnished identically in everything but color: where one had green bedspreads, curtains, sheets, carpeting, towels, and lampshades, the others had blue, red, or gold. Only the clutter of clothes, toys, and sports equipment assured me that the rooms were occupied by actual children with distinct personalities. One upstairs closet was entirely filled with children's gifts, wrapped in advance and ready to be given out at the birthday parties the boys attended. Barbara stored household products in bulk, but she didn't save mementos or trinkets; there were almost no family photographs or children's art projects in the house. Even the glamorous furnishings, I found, had been bought all at once, in a single trip to the Bloomingdale's design department. Barbara did not have a junk drawer, and she did not need one. She simply put categorizable things in their proper places and threw odd and uncategorizable things away.

After school each day, Barbara's sons shuttled through a cycle of lessons and play dates, which gave Barbara time for tennis and let me clean the house in peace. She left me snacks, kept the pantry stocked with cleaning supplies—bags for three different kinds of vacuum cleaners, a special polish for the stainless steel range—and let me know, with unconflicted candor, when I forgot a job. Aside from that, I spent most of my days in the Robbins house alone.

I moved through the rooms in silence, daydreaming, savoring the smooth, cool, knobby shapes of the netsuke, the unexpectedly bristly nap of the zebra rug, the glossy salami-speckled marble on top of the bombé chests. As the months went on and I grew quicker at my tasks, I filled in the spare minutes happily, mostly by surreptitious reading. From Barbara's bookshelves I plucked down Bruno Bettelheim and Freud, David Reuben's *Everything You Ever Wanted to Know About Sex* and textbooks on psychology, the novels of Bellow, Updike, Roth, even Genet. Nosing under the boys' beds, the vacuum occasionally unearthed troves of cheap pornography, crudely explicit tales of horny hitchhikers and lusty suburban wives. I read those avidly too, half aroused and half incredulous, edified and misled.

Over the six years I worked for her, Barbara and I built an odd relationship, not quite close yet somehow deeply necessary to us both. A daughter by proxy in her household of men, I checked the evenness of her hems, gave her bath beads on her birthday, admired the plain expensive dresses she bought for her frequent evenings out. She gave me art books and dictionaries for Christmas and talked to me about my college plans. The school I eventually chose was Barbara's alma mater, a place already familiar to me from her recollections, her yearbooks, and her advice.

My mother and Barbara met occasionally over the years, chatting for a minute or two when they bumped into each other in Shop-Rite or when Barbara dropped me off at home after work. My mother liked Barbara well enough, though I suspect her new role as mother of the maid felt odd. I was busy enough outside of our house to let up on the undeclared war I was waging on my mother within it, but I idolized the Robbinses and I let it show. One afternoon my mother finally lost her temper. "Why don't you just go live there, already?" she said. "Let Barbara adopt you. She's the mother you always wanted, anyway." We were standing in our kitchen, that friendly, central, slightly messy room, faced off across the linoleum floor like boxers at the end of a long bout. The makings of dinner were on the counter near the stove, and our poodle was snuffling contentedly at his bowl. It was a terrifying moment, mostly because what she said was true.

True, but not, I think now, in the way that both of us feared. I did not actually want the real person that Barbara was for a mother. What I wanted, fiercely, was a mother whose whose example I could live up to, whose shoes I could fill. I felt myself to be less patient and less accepting than my own mother, less adaptable, less generous, and less fun. I feared myself to be less loving and less feminine too. What Barbara proved to me was that I could make a sufficient life without my mother's gifts and attractions. Barbara was a woman I could someday be. Disciplined, capable, smart, pleasant; a little eccentric, but not intolerably weird. Attractive, if not really pretty; affectionate, if not truly warm. A brain, if not a heart as well. That was what she offered, just that sense of achievability. The art books and college advice she gave me worked just like my mother's lipsticked kisses once had. They were badges of membership, assurances that I was not a misfit, confirmations that I carried on some maternal tradition, some female line.

I went to college and, wrapped up in my life there, lost touch with the Robbinses. Slowly my relationship with my mother steadied and settled. I began to see that we were not quite as different as I'd feared. When I got an apartment of my own, she and I finally rebuilt our domestic alliance. She went with me when I scoured flea markets for sturdy old furniture and nice old prints, and helped me paint my kitchen yellow, and never came to visit without bringing some characteristically inexpensive and festive little gift. Once more I had the chance to enjoy her gift for improvisation, this time in my own small home.

Both my mother and Barbara—those two mothers, those two keepers of houses—have a powerful symbolic presence in my home. My flea market finds, my refinished and adapted furniture, the dinners I improvise with take-out food on pretty china all celebrate my mother's spirit. Barbara's legacy lives in my neat closets, the supplies and foodstuffs I buy and store in advance, my carefully ordered and alphabetized files. As my mother used to (in retirement, without children underfoot, she has become more attentive to small domestic details), I tend to let dust balls settle under the couch and ice build up in the freezer, saving time for more pleasurable pursuits than cleaning. Like Barbara I throw out inessentials, extras, and leftovers of all kinds, from old clothes to unused Christmas cards. I have a junk drawer full of odd and unaccountable things, but it's more timid— less exuberantly crowded, more self-conscious—than my mother's, and every six months or so I clean it out and start from scratch again.

Until a few years ago I would have said that the extremes of possibility these two women represented defined my house and my housekeeping. Lately I've grown less sure. Belatedly it has occurred to me that my mother and Barbara are not really opposites in the way I'd always thought. Underneath their superficial differences they share something fundamental. Both are realists, and both have the realist's instinctive understanding that something always has to be sacrificed. Barbara sacrificed the pizzazz, the spontaneity, the fun, the creativity of her home. My mother sacrificed the control, the perfection, the pure and comforting order. Both of them lived at peace with their choice, and with the necessity for making it.

Unlike them, I'm not in the least a realist. The domestic goddess, the muse, the model, the ancestress, the symbolic mother of my home is in fact my father. It makes no difference that he never cooked a meal or dusted a shelf; it is his temperament, and his idealistic sense of what a home should be, that is most alive in mine.

My father and I are not at peace with our domestic compromises. We are not, at heart, compromisers at all. We get anxious over our homes in a way neither my mother nor Barbara ever do, and sometimes we are driven to fury at the limits of the world, the impossibility of being everything at once, the unwillingness of other people to live up to the ideal orders we devise. We are ambitious for ourselves and our houses. We love to make improvements and we tire ourselves out with them, so that we end up having too little energy or too little time for the world outside the home, which both my mother and Barbara Robbins love and savor. My father and I both adore our houses, but we live in them a little uneasily. We both acknowledge the miscellaneousness of the world by making ourselves a junk drawer, but we never really manage to like it.

Bedroom One

I learned about the connection between sex and rooms and

loss and foreignness when I was fifteen, watching a Saturday

matinee showing of *Doctor Zhivago* at the Park Theatre. Happily ignorant that I was being educated, I lost myself in the film with unself-conscious rapture. The Park, now demolished to make way for a regional bank, was a movie palace in the old style. The leaded-glass lamps cast a dim and somber light, the thick plush curtain rustled open and shut between films, and along the walls stood a line of plaster goddesses looking nubile but uneasy. I sat in the ornate gloom reveling in the absence of a proprietary parent or sibling, letting the epic movements of the film wash over me, and feeling myself much too sophisticated for the large-size box of Milk Duds I secretly craved.

Today *Doctor Zhivago* strikes me as vastly overblown, but at fifteen I welcomed its excesses, which assured me that it was Art and not mere entertainment. When the movie ended and I stumbled out into the bright banal glare beyond the marquee, I felt for the first time the disorientation that sometimes follows transformative moments, a blank dizziness that signals an imagined world grown suddenly vivid and an everyday reality gone suddenly flat.

I saw the movie five times, played "Lara's Theme" endlessly on the piano, pumping the damper pedal hard, and wrote a paper for my theater arts class about Zhivago's balalaika as a symbol of generational connection. It felt like part of my burgeoning adulthood to have figured out what a symbol was and to have identified one in the wild. I was less astute when it came to the film's broader metaphors: the images that moved my emotions, the aesthetic threads that tied Russians, sex, and revolution to my uneventful adolescence in a small New Jersey town. There's a clue, maybe, in the fact that when I watched the film again last month I found I'd forgotten huge chunks of the narrative but remembered the sets exactly, right down to the round bellies of the oil lamps and the sunflowers languorously shedding their petals in the field hospital's dusty sun.

The rooms are so *romantic*, I would say back then, savoring the look of them on my second or third or fourth viewing. What I meant, though it didn't quite break through to my consciousness, was that they are sexual. The flat of Lara's mother, for example, is a warren of elaborate laces, ball-fringed cushions, curly brass beds, and shapely dressmaker dummies. Sensual and fussily anxious, its tangle of corridors—bordered by grimy, translucent windows—lend it a secretive air at odds with its bourgeois respectability. It's a place in which the right hand never quite knows whom the left hand is touching, where too much is seen and too much hidden at the same time. The restaurants and private alcoves to which Komarovsky takes Lara share the same belle époque ambiance, but there it's stripped of its feminine sham propriety. Their red velvet fittings, mirrors, and gilded statues are overtly voluptuous, ponderously and blatantly seductive.

The secrets embedded in these imaginary spaces made me anxious when I first watched the film. I was happier when, later in the story, other rooms countered their tainted sexuality. The farmer's cottage on the Varykino estate, simple and fecund, and Lara's clean whitewashed apartment in Yuriatin seemed reassuringly untainted to me. The movie's last home is the disused manor house at Varykino, to which Lara and Zhivago move for their final, brief reunion. In it the past of family life, sexual warmth, and aristocratic culture has been literally stopped. The chairs are slipcovered in snow, the chandeliers glitter with ice, and the windows wear frost's lacy curtains. Life there has frozen into an extra-human purity that needs to be awakened, like a domestic Sleeping Beauty, with the heat of a lover's kiss. Not surprisingly, this gorgeously dormant space was my favorite of the film's many and elaborate rooms.

The interiors in the film suggest shamefully fulfilling sex, procreative marital sex, ecstatically redemptive sex—they're about sexual character, states of sexual experience. Interiors in Caldwell, New Jersey, in the 1960s were about many things—expedience, convention, and middle-class aspiration among them—but they weren't about sex. It was a revelation to find that the two could be connected: that the tactile and visual stimulations of sex aren't entirely different from those of drapes and love seats, that sexuality can influence the mood and textures of a room, that a room itself can excite and intensify desire. Another surprise was the sheer variety of the film's spaces, the multiplicity of possibilities. I didn't know how to express all of this back then, and I didn't quite understand it. But I got it, as we used to say, on a gut level—and it electrified me. No wonder I stumbled drunkenly as I walked out of the Park Theatre that afternoon. The world had become much wider and considerably more perverse while I was inside.

Doctor Zhivago is a movie in the great romantic tradition, a movie about longing rather than fulfillment. Even as a teenager I sensed that it was filled with lost Edens: spaces that once housed grace, places that could only briefly be reclaimed before they would be lost once again. Again and again I noticed the film's characters glimpse a warm room through a pane of glass from the street outside (one of the novel's most famous images is that of a candle that, burning, melts a window's white obscuring frost), or through a glass panel—variously etched, shaped, and frosted—inside the room itself. Like me, Zhivago and his intimates seemed like voyeurs in their own lives, staring hungrily at what they need most to live.

I understood this completely, though I pretended to myself that I didn't. I didn't want to know that what connected me to the people in the film was not their romance but their isolation. The way they were always just missing one another. The way, despite all their passions, they were ultimately abandoned, lost, left. The way their story began with a child losing a parent and ended with the death of an adult, alone, on a bleak and anonymous street.

Though I didn't want to acknowledge it, the film moved me precisely because I so powerfully understood what it was like to feel myself on the outside of warm rooms looking in—to glimpse what I deeply desired through a barrier sometimes warmed to transparency but never broken through. I didn't want to acknowledge that the film had introduced me to how beautiful rooms could be and how inevitably they were lost, or to understand that those gorgeous lost rooms were emblems of love. I didn't want to abandon myself to the abandonments of passion, or to see sex not as love or destiny but as an urgent rush to exist for a moment within those warm enclosures—to melt the false, defensive social skin of frost and ice.

I may not have wanted any of these things, but the movie gave me permission to *want* to want them—to make room in my life for excess, risk, loss, some kind of revelation. The interiors of *Doctor Zhivago* made all of this tremble fruitfully right on the edge of my consciousness. They let me experience the kind of desire I needed, an intimation of longing that didn't force me too fast toward fulfillment.

The longings I half felt seeing *Doctor Zhivago* in the Park Theatre weren't fulfilled until more than a decade later, when I spent four weeks in Paris. At first I was startled, wandering around the streets of the Sixth Arrondissement or watching people stroll through the Tuileries, to find myself remembering the Russian rooms in an old movie that I had learned to find a bit ridiculous. Then I realized that the film's murmurs of isolation and foreignness, excess and physicality, transience and persistence were finding an echo, delayed but clear, amid those Parisian places. In some odd way, living imaginatively in the rooms of the film at fifteen had marked the start of my adolescence. Living in Paris that October marked its end. The movie awakened in me a tentative consent to a kind of desire, and the four weeks of my stay in Paris helped me let it go.

I had gone to Paris to visit my friend Liz, who was studying art history there. From the moment I entered the airport taxi, dubiously muttering *"vingt-et-un, rue des Vieux Colombiers"* like an agnostic's prayer, it was obvious that here, as in the film, the past was a place to be inhabited. With its formal, pearly skyline and its tatters of faded posters, its intricate storefronts and its mournful allées, its curves of lace curtain and its panes of etched and frosted glass, Paris had an old, layered gorgeousness. Its age made me feel insignificant, an oddly liberating sensation. Surrounded by the voluptuous evidence of survival and loss, free from the inhibiting common sense of home, I suddenly felt the caution I'd always been proud of to be a hedged and defensive thing.

By the time the taxi jolted to a stop in front of Liz's building, in the rue des Vieux Colombiers, a narrow street in the shadow of Saint-Sulpice, I was already prepared to let that caution go. Number 21 was a big, shabby old structure. At the street level a patisserie sat next to a lesbian bar called Katmandu. Liz's apartment was on the top floor, up seven tightly curling flights of wooden steps so old they bowed in the middle. The tiny lamps on each landing stayed on almost long enough to light me to the next and then extinguished themselves, leaving the stairs behind in thick, soft darkness.

Reaching Liz's door was like leaving earth behind, like climbing to heaven on foot.

Liz's apartment was a studio, rented out by a mediocre French artist at great profit to a succession of American graduate students. It was long and narrow, with slanted skylights and a north wall composed entirely of windows. It held a wooden rack of badly painted canvases; a lumpy bed with a worm-eaten Gothic altarpiece, probably faked, at its head; a wine-stained, cigarette-scarred wooden table; and a small bookcase packed with English paperback mysteries, the endearing legacy of years of homesick American youths.

The place had the sleepy beauty of the rooms of *Zhivago* and all of the inconveniences epic films ignore. Heated only by a small electric stove, it was cold until the brief afternoon hour when the sharply angled autumn sun slanted into the room. At night, lying on a makeshift pallet of old curtains and spare blankets, I could feel currents of chilly air drift and eddy around me and see the stars through the skylight far above. At the opposite end of the apartment, Liz, lying in greater comfort on her bed, seemed unaffected by either the cold or the stars above the skylights. The kitchen consisted of a closet holding a plug-in kettle, a tiny refrigerator, and a hot plate with a single grimy ring. We ate out or brought home croissants baked in the patisserie downstairs, ham and sausage, cheese, wine, fruit. The bathroom window disclosed a postcard-sized view, toylike and distant, of the Eiffel Tower. The supply of water that reached the shower was meager and icy. I washed each night from kettle-boiled water

I poured into the bathroom sink. Like an awkward, ungenerous stripper, I stood in my warm sweat suit and uncovered each small patch of flesh in turn—first baring it, then scrubbing it, then rubbing it dry, and finally covering it up again.

These minor humiliations of the flesh were also reminders of it. I had never been so aware of the dense creaminess of cheese, the metallic aftertaste of warmish red wine, the restlessness of the eddying night air, the tender goosefleshed skin of my ribs under the rough washcloth. I felt electric with unfamiliar discomfort. The city that stretched sensuously around the apartment seemed to be charged with physicality. Down pillows smelled sharply of fowl; milk, of the farmyard. Hares still in their glossy pelts hung from striped shop awnings. The air was freighted with the smell of river, black decaying leaf, perfume, exhaust, strong cigarettes. The people looked wiry, intense, and sexual. Even the buildings seemed to have palpable flesh, tender and crumbling, folded into curves and hidden corners, blushing in the thin autumn sun.

Liz, who spent her time in the archives of the Bibliothèque Nationale, was a comforting but mostly invisible presence. I woke in the morning to an empty studio filled with milky light, then went out to walk around the city, sometimes toward the fixed destination of a museum or park, but more often without a plan. What pleased me weren't the so-called attractions but the textures of the ordinary things, the big anonymous buildings, the half-empty squares. The old gravel courtyard of the Palais Royal, its arcades lined with shops selling military medals. An unremarkable café in the Marais, where I drank my coffee next to three old women in rusty black dresses who seemed oblivious to the flock of rapacious pigeons that fluttered around their feet. The Marie de Médicis fountain in the Jardin du Luxembourg, a mournful narrow pool lined by swags of ivy. The Montmartre cemetery, where I was startled by the marauding cats and moved by the sight of a hundred nameless mausoleums falling ungently to pieces. These places and people seemed both beautiful and strange to me, literally foreign, as if I was ignorant not just of the place's spoken language but also its civic, human, and architectural ones as well.

It was the first time in my life I had ever spent more than a day with no fixed obligations or schedule, accountable to no one but myself, with no one knowing where I was. There was no place easy or familiar to rest during those days, no longstanding habit to make me feel anchored. Rootless and truant, I wandered the streets dressed just well enough to be inconspicuous, making no impression on the places or people I passed. It was strange to feel at once so edgily alive and so invisible—to feel myself so energetic, to find myself as effectless as a ghost.

Without a command of the language, without companions, I rarely had the courage to engage in the life of the city. Like the characters in *Doctor Zhivago*, I saw what I wanted— an antique paisley shawl, a wedge of peppered chèvre, a man with beautiful hands and a clever, long-boned face—through the glass panes of café windows, apartment facades, storefronts. I stood on the outside of a corner bistro filled with laughter and argument, a shop in which sheets of paper were marbled in tubs of oily pigment, an *antiquaire*'s with grey-green walls and a silk-lined Empire daybed. I looked inside fiercely, startled by the intensity of longing these places filled me with.

At the end of my first week, Liz brought me to a party crowded with expatriates and students. I wore a short black dress and felt confident, reckless. I met an Englishman named Joe at the party. A year or so younger than I was, he had the slender, slightly unformed face of a boy. He wore oddly formal, wonderfully tailored clothes and wire-rimmed spectacles. He was intelligent and sweet of temperament. I was infatuated with Joe, and also with the unexplored possibilities of myself.

With Joe, who spoke impeccable French, I entered the rooms of the city for a few charmed weeks. In his company I understood the labels of the dusty Musée Nissim de Camondo, bought the paisley shawl, bargained at the Puces flea market unafraid, ate at a restaurant near the Beaux-Arts as confidently as any other diner. Joe lived in a pension, one of the small, ramshackle hotels—a warren of narrow halls and rooms that were barely more than cells—clustered around Saint-Germain-des-Prés. His room was papered with faded roses. Headlights from the rue Jacob flickered through its tall window. We lay each evening in the narrow bed listening to the sounds, the stories that bled through the tissue-thin walls: the groan as a man in the next room settled himself to bed, the anxious half-audible pleadings of a younger man down the hall begging a lover not to leave him. We talked idly, quietly, and we made love. Our lovemaking wasn't a rapturous merging or an explosive release. It felt like a tender, fumbling attempt to move beyond the warm dense barriers of our bodies, to dwell for a moment in another's vulnerable, fleshly space.

If I had been a character in a movie like *Zhivago*, I might have felt sated and languorous. Instead, in meeting Joe I fell from the newborn electricity of my lonely first week straight into a state of foreboding. To be persistently on the outside of things, however lonely it felt, had given me an odd anticipatory freedom. When everything was possible, nothing could be lost. Lying in that tiny room off the Boulevard Saint-Germain, pressed too close to Joe's not-quite-familiar body, uneasily full of more wine and food than I was used to, I lost that adolescent carelessness, that willed unconsciousness of risk.

Now that I was inside the city's glowing rooms, all I could think of was how soon I would be unceremoniously ushered out of them: expelled back into the world of New York, of bills and responsibilities, of fixed routines, of ordinary rather than glamorous discomfort. Now that I had a small claim on Paris I felt less romantically invigorated by it—I felt worried, prematurely bereft. The crumbling of the *hôtels particuliers* seemed ominous, an emblem of my inevitable unhousing. The sight of Joe's animated, intelligent face over a Kir in the café was a painful pleasure, a guarantee of loss.

Thirty days after I arrived hesitantly in Paris, I flew home to New York. Manhattan felt as unfamiliar to me as if I had been gone for years. The light was flat and glaring, the urban landscape dirtily grey, the scale of the city inhumanly large. Everything seemed incomprehensibly foreign, with a brutal strangeness I did not want to face. I cried as the cab bucked and rushed over the potholes of the FDR Drive, pulling my paisley shawl around my shoulders, feeling unready and bereft.

At the end of *Doctor Zhivago*, Lara abandons her country and Zhivago abandons her. Both of them survive, but they lose their Eden. In the film these losses are heroic; their tragedies are destiny. This is what draws us into darkened theaters to watch epic films, the seductive way they frame heartbreak as something grand, something romantic.

In that kind of movie, loss is gorgeous, luminous, redemptive. In real life, in the bright sun outside the dim old-fashioned cave of the theater, loss is usually just loss, and it is ordinary, unremarkable, part of the natural order of things, a by-product mostly of unrelated choices. I returned to New York because I had a paid-for ticket and business to do, because America was by chance my home, because the unromantic minutiae of ordinary existence can be put off only so long. Joe stopped writing to me, a year or so later, because his own everyday life absorbed him, took him back in. I haven't gone back to Paris, which I loved, because other plans and destinations have used up my money and my time. In the end, it's all just as well. As I finally let *Doctor Zhivago* show me, the foreignness of another place or another soul can't really be inhabited. It can only be lost: because you leave it or because, as you stay on, time dilutes its strangeness with familiarity and brings you home again.

Bedroom Two

I spent most of my early twenties longing to have my own

apartment and most of my middle twenties longing to get

out of it. Once I found an affordable place, a studio on the edgy northern boundary of Manhattan's Upper East Side, I spent hours decorating it with flea market armchairs, rag rugs, a series of sepia photographs composed with artistic vagueness, a chic ficus tree in a terra-cotta pot, and a bed, optimistically double, which took up a full quarter of the available floor space. I bought pillow shams and guest towels, a typewriter and a file cube, dinnerware, cookbooks, and spices. It didn't occur to me that living alone was, like gourmet cooking, a process that required not only good ingredients but also patience, creativity, and skill. Without those psychic supplies, my apartment was hideously lonely. Too proud to admit my fears or my failure, unsupported as yet by the new friends I'd hoped to meet, I turned with relief to the expedient of dating. Even the numbing banality of the worst date was preferable to an evening spent alone at home eating leftover pasta, rereading *Jane Eyre* or Jane Austen, and listening to the valedictory *click* of dying ficus leaves hitting my lovingly polished wooden floor.

None of the dates I had for the first year or so flowered into anything more than a mild liking. Now, fifteen years later, my memories of those men are vague, though their homes remain fresh in my mind. Trying to recall the men without the apartments is like trying to remember the words of a poem without their cadence.

Arthur, with his meticulous lime green kitchen and cross-word-patterned shower curtain. Jack, whose high-rise penthouse was strewn with dirty shirts, *Playboy* magazines, beer bottles, and an expensive telescope trained on the windows of the skyscraper next door. Maurice, who lived in a rather grand co-op off Fifth Avenue and collected Art Deco; and Andy, who lived up six flights of stairs in the pseudo-bohemian squalor of a tenement on East Tenth, the first home I'd ever seen with a bathtub in the kitchen. The freshness and persistence of these images tells me that the information these apartments offered—about the lives of men, or life in Manhattan, or the art of living alone—must have been more interesting and more necessary to me than the men themselves. At the time, though, I strenuously resisted my urge to analyze the meaning of these homes. I felt guilty when I found myself mentally wrinkling up my nose at Jack's adolescent fantasy pad or wondering whether Andy's soul was as drab and stingy as his rooms. I didn't question either my fascination or my denial; I simply went on feeling, in some confused and half-conscious way, that to judge a man by his dinnerware or curtains was unacceptably materialistic, as superficial as judging him by the shape of his face, the maker of his suit, or the name of his alma mater.

A stockbroker who had recently moved from San Francisco to New York changed my mind. Philip (the Wall Street colleague who introduced us confided reverently) had discussed trends in debt on *Wall Street Week in Review*, been quoted in *Barron's*, and been invited to breakfast by Michael Milken, in the halcyon days before dining chez Milken required the permission of a warden. In person, this buccaneer of bonds had the gangly, rawboned frame of Abe Lincoln, the freckles of Tom Sawyer, and an endearingly bashful, plain-spoken manner. I fell in love with Philip more or less immediately, enchanted by the gap between the man he seemed to be and the slick, fast-talking, Hermès-tied horror he might so easily have been instead.

Within a month, Philip and I were spending four or five nights a week together, always in my apartment. No longer lonely there, I bought new sheets and abandoned the skeletal ficus in favor of bunches of bright tulips. Cheerfully Philip curled his lanky body into my too-short bed and stooped under my too-low shower. He was affectionate, tender, and in some indefinable way vague. So strong were my need and my nesting instinct that it was weeks before I realized that his failure to invite me to his apartment—not to mention his failure to explain *why* he wasn't inviting me there—was the result, not of chance, but of conscious evasion. Teetering between euphoria and paranoia on the seesaw of love, I found myself as unable to voice my confusion as I was to stop speculating on its source. What was he hiding in the Riverside Drive apartment he mentioned but never shared? The most lurid, and for some reason most compelling, of my imaginings was a kind of Bertha Rochester fantasy, in which Philip had a mad first wife cached away, not among English battlements but in an airy Manhattan penthouse with a terrace, an eat-in kitchen, and a stunning river view.

One sleeting December afternoon Philip and I found ourselves stranded, cab- and umbrellaless, a mere block from where he said he lived. With the gloom of a man fresh out of excuses, he led me through his lobby, nodded in response to the doorman's bland smile, unlocked his apartment door, and ushered me into a huge space dramatically lit by the greenish flashes of the storm. There was no mad wife inside. In fact, there was nothing inside at all, except maybe some of the least-fettered dust balls this side of Waco. In his eight months of tenancy, Philip had furnished his three-bedroom, two-bath, fourteen-hundred-square-foot apartment with a king-sized mattress, a mattress frame, a television, a television stand, an unpainted pine kitchen stool, and enough stacked copies of the *Wall Street Journal* to almost make a table, sort of. As we walked through the empty, eerie rooms, Philip began to mumble something that might have been an explanation. Giddy with relief, as anxious as ever not to conflate character and home furnishing, I didn't listen. As enthusiastically as I had secretly suspected him, I hurried to exonerate Philip of any fault worse than a sweetly befuddled and endearingly male asceticism.

This, alas, was a mistake. My unconscious had the last laugh. Philip, it transpired, did have a wife, who lived in San Francisco, along, presumably, with his furniture. She was not mad, but she was angry as hell. And so was I, though it took me six more months of hope and misery before I could acknowledge it, even to myself.

Philip and I split up in May. I spent much of the summer that followed alone in my apartment. For the first time it felt like a haven, a place of comfort and healing, a home. During those oppressive summer months, Philip's vacant rooms came often to my mind, emblems of his irresolution and my powers of denial. Somehow, for all my anxious speculation over his secrets and intentions, the questions his apartment raised hadn't engaged my mind. I hadn't wondered how he could live for so long in its emptiness—without a painting or print on the wall, a table for a meal, a chair from which to watch the light fade over the river—or what that emptiness said about his readiness to root himself in his new hometown. I hadn't asked myself why this lack of color, texture, and comfort—this monastic self-denial in the service of no visible god—didn't trouble him. I hadn't even noticed the unlikeliness of our pairing, that mating between an obsessive nest builder and a bird who seemed content to perch awkwardly, forever, on bare rock.

The truth, I realized that summer, was that I *had* judged Philip superficially. I had read courage in the bluntness of his jaw and wisdom in the rueful tone of his voice. To judge him by his home would have been less, not more, shallow than interpreting these genetic givens. Like random lines on a page, Philip's physical being had an attractiveness entirely arbitrary, unconnected to meaning. His rooms, in contrast, spoke a language that was subtle and unconsciously systematic, rich with intention, complexity, and choice, the last tellingly avoided if not engaged. The meanings of Philip's rooms were connotative, not denotative—suggestive rather than direct. But how relevant was their evidence about the imperatives, physical and emotional, of love; how germane their glimpse of a private self; how apropos their information on habits of body and gifts of mind.

The notion that men use rooms to romance women has long been part of the popular imagination. A novel written in 1752, Jean-François Bastide's *La Petite Maison*, tells the story of how the Marquis de Trémicourt seduces a courtesan named Mélite by leading her through the rooms of his "love nest," a small house built on the banks of the Seine. She finally succumbs in the boudoir; its "walls are entirely lined with looking-glass, and the joins between them have been hidden by false tree trunks, with carefully arranged branches and leaves." Bastide's description of these undeniably sensuous rooms is profusely, almost perversely, detailed, but the same general idea is still current today, so familiar it's become a cliché. Every adolescent knows that the way to what one might loosely call a woman's heart leads through a room filled with low light, soft couches, and a bar stocked with strong drink.

There is no corresponding popular wisdom for women. No body of novels, stories, or songs that I know of encourages us to use our own sensitivity to place to read a man through his rooms, to pay attention to our own comfort level and perceptions there, to assert our own form of control. The closest we get is a literature peppered with women who can't, or don't, read the writing on the walls. Clarissa is one. As my unconscious informed me, Jane Eyre is another. Intelligent as she is, the jarring gloom and locked attics of Thornfield Hall barely faze her. I could have used some more-empowering models. I was savvy enough to guard myself against the clichéd seducer with his cocktail shaker and dimmer switch, but when it came to men like Philip, men who expressed in their rooms a more complex and contradictory agenda than simple fast sex, I didn't have—or more accurately, I had but didn't use—a clue.

Thinking about this failure gave me a new perspective on my earlier dates, too. It told me that my distaste for Andy and Jack, like my fears about Philip, had been not meretricious judgments but readings—acute ones—of texts that I'd simply refused to acknowledge were in front of my eyes. I finally realized, too, that of the Manhattan homes I had seen, the rooms that spoke most strongly of stability and pleasure, comfort and delight, were my own.

Several years after I last saw Philip, I met James. Like Philip a stockbroker, James appeared to be his antithesis. Tan and handsome, with blue eyes and gleaming, dark hair, he seemed too suave to be trustworthy. A week after our first date, he invited me to a dinner party at his apartment. It was a penthouse in a good old building in the East Seventies, but at first sight it was not a reassuring place. The walls and high ceilings were shadowed with soot, the parquet floors dull, the tables and chairs a motley and cat-clawed assortment left over from James's recent divorce. With tattered shreds of wallpaper peeling from its walls and a neat round hole where its doorknob should have been, the bathroom had the derelict air of the early stages of a renovation, though nothing in it would ever get fixed in the years I knew James. The drapes in the bedroom were so old that the sun had rotted both fabric and lining, leaving a fretwork of tiny tears.

James's must have been the only apartment in New York where you could watch the sun set over the Manhattan skyline through—instead of between—the drapes.

But James's apartment functioned beautifully, like a good syllogism couched in awkward language. The experience, unlike the look, of it was one of efficiency and ease. The Baldwin baby grand piano in the corner of the living room was in perfect tune, the bookcases densely and neatly filled, the expensive scale in the bathroom perfectly calibrated (James's streak of vanity was not small). The tiny kitchen was organized with the painstaking efficiency of a yacht's galley. The wing chairs and couches, though threadbare, seated the twelve guests in genuine comfort.

James had chosen a good red wine and cooked a savory *bœuf bourguignon* in a stew pot he'd inherited from his mother and preserved, through scrupulous scouring and seasoning, for twenty years. We ate on a rusty iron table on his narrow brick terrace under the intense lapis blue of the New York sky, surrounded by a profusion of trees and roses James had meticulously tended, and accompanied by strains of Mozart emanating from the stereo inside. Lit by the dancing candlelight, the incongruities of the rickety chairs and mismatched dishes faded into insignificance. The conversation was lively and disputatious, and James made a solicitous host. By the time I left the party, at 2 A.M., sated and pleasantly sleepy, I had realized that both apartment and man were more complex, and more domestic, than they seemed.

James, I came to realize in the years I spent with him, inhabited his apartment the same way he experienced his life, intensely and idiosyncratically. He was passionate about his particular interests, which were diverse and eccentric, and meticulous about the workings of everything from his fireplace to his kitchen faucet. About everything else he didn't, as he inelegantly put it, give a rat's ass. He had, in that way, an aristocratic rather than a middle-class sensibility, an innate sense of personal entitlement that bordered on the arrogant. The flouting of status and convention in his apartment reflected this—the place had a swashbuckling, shabby, unrehearsed grandeur. Both James and his apartment were sometimes angering and often disconcerting. There was a species of ruthlessness in both. But James's home, like James, had an exuberance as well—a measure of vigor and appetite, a lack of self-consciousness—that was potently sexy. So were the sheer confidence, the refusal to stoop to the indirect seduction or the calculated charm, that they both shared.

Chastened by the debacle of Philip, I tried to pay attention to these complicated signs: not judging or keeping score, just observing. I noticed how resolutely James refused to invest in the symbols and compromises of domestic ties, as well as how passionately he lived. I noticed his home's carelessness as well as its comforts. I acknowledged his willingness to share his home with me, but I also saw how little impact my tastes or interests made on it as the years went on. I tried to picture myself making a life there, but I failed. The quieter, prettier precincts of my own apartment always felt like a necessary corrective; like a foreign city, the wonders and pleasures of James's apartment never came to feel like home. None of these observations were consciously on my mind when I told James I wouldn't marry him, three years or so after I first entered his apartment, but they informed my decision, were one of the subtexts of my words.

James and I are still friends. He married recently, bringing his bride to live in the same Seventy-sixth Street apartment that I knew. A few months after the wedding, during a quick weekday lunch, he invited me over to see the newly renovated space. I walked behind him through the lobby, past the surprised face of the familiar elevator man, feeling just a little like the proverbial other woman. Inside, the apartment had been transformed. The walls and ceiling were immaculately white and adorned with new crown moldings, baseboards, built-in cabinetry. The floors had been polished, the old furniture covered—I could just make out the plump, well-worn shapes—with taupe linen crisply piped in blue. There were lamps with pleated silk shades, needlepoint cushions, even a new mahogany dining table with six matching chairs. The walls of the bathroom were slick with glossy green lacquer, and its door boasted an antique brass doorknob with a pretty braided trim.

At first I was disappointed. How bland this attractive, civilized interior seemed in comparison to James's once-ramshackle home. How much less engaging was this prettiness than the former contradictory vigor. How small an achievement it felt, suddenly, to have drapes beautifully made of neat Schumacher toile. The new apartment, so much more like everyone else's than it was like James's, seemed to me to represent a dampening of James's passions, an abandonment of James's self.

But as we walked through the rooms I began to suspect, just as I had on the balmy evening of James's dinner party ten years before, that my first impression was wrong. Maybe the flood tide of James's energy hadn't dried up but merely been rerouted. Maybe he had simply decided to include a woman within the charmed circle reserved for his scrupulous attention. Maybe the apartment's new, neat prettiness was not tamed or timid, but tender: a gesture of respect for Beth's needs and sensibilities, an acknowledgment of the care and compromises necessary to make his partnership with her work as smoothly as his kitchen or his stereo. I didn't leave James's apartment with deep regret. I had long made peace with our incompatibility; I had also recognized, belatedly, the possibilities of my own life. But I did leave James's house rueful. For all the uncompromising certainty of James's bachelor rooms, they had been—like all things human— susceptible to change, filled with the possibility of growth. For all the painstaking care of my observations, James would have made a better husband than I'd thought.

Dining Room

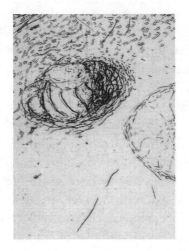

Each time I visit my parents in Florida I spend an after-

noon or two having tea with my grandmother, who lives on

the other side of town. Her house is cluttered with the

detritus of old age and illness—misplaced hearing aids, prescription pill bottles, aluminum walkers, doctor's bills—but our teas are meticulously formal. We sit across from each other at the lace-covered table, drinking milky Earl Grey from gold-rimmed Minton cups and eating the shortbread biscuits she has fanned out on an oval cut-glass server. My grandfather, at ninety-six grown tired and abstracted, sits in the adjoining sun porch watching whatever ball game is on TV. While we eat we can hear his muttered comments on bad calls and, sometimes, the strained, wheezing breathing of his sleep.

Our conversation is as familiar as our place settings. I ask my grandmother about their health, fish for news of the other grandchildren. Is cousin Nancy's second husband nice? How is Joe and Betty's new daughter? She asks about my work and my social life. Have I met anyone special lately? she always inquires delicately. No one special, I always say. I've learned from past experience that her apparently vague question refers quite specifically to suitable men of marriageable age, steady disposition, and serious intentions. I appreciate her interest, but no longer try to explain either the complicated gavotte that is modern dating or my own ambivalent response to it.

Behind my grandmother as we talk stands a large mahogany breakfront filled with Royal Bayreuth pitchers, Limoges cups, and a set of eight formal dessert plates, which arc over her head like frivolous halos. Made by Haviland a century or so ago, the plates have plain white centers surrounded by bands of pure deep pink. Their rims are swagged with gold leaves suspended between knots of tiny cobalt, emerald, and crimson flowers. They are decorative but not fussy, feminine but not girlish, delicate but without the curlicues and flourishes of so much painted china. I notice these plates particularly, not only because they are beautiful but because they are, in a manner of speaking, mine: my right, and in a way, my failure.

Ten years ago, when the plates first appeared in the breakfront, I asked my grandmother enviously where she got them. "From a dealer," she said. "They're for your wedding present," she added, her voice uncolored by irony, humor, or doubt. She has held to that purpose ever since. My failure to announce approaching nuptials doesn't trouble her. Nor does the passage of the years. She is as loyal to the possibility of my marriage and the appropriateness of the plates to its celebration as a faithful believer is to life after death.

So long promised and so long withheld, these plates make me feel affectionate, annoyed, and childishly resistant. I'm delighted by their splendor and irritated by the way they rest on their shelves uselessly, year after year, like overdressed wallflowers sitting out an endless cotillion. I'm amused by my grandmother's stubbornness, and appalled by the possibility that, given her age and frailty—she's ninety-four this year—I'll end up receiving these gorgeous plates as her legacy rather than as her gift. I have found no workable language in which to express these feelings. The closest I've come is to ask her, teasingly, if she would consider a deal:

would she promise to give me the plates either at my wedding or on my fortieth birthday, whichever came first? She laughed at this but said nothing. If she heard the tension behind the ostensibly lighthearted words, she gave no sign.

There's no doubt in my mind that my grandmother loves me deeply. In some ways she knows me well: her choice of those plates, which answer my passion for both splendor and order, is proof of that. In other ways I'm invisible to her. Conforming to none of the known contours of her experience, my life is unrecognizable terrain, an exotic country in which she has never traveled. How could she know my landmarks? She has never felt the euphoria of signing the papers that purchased her own home with her own earnings, or lain awake wondering if those earnings alone will be enough to keep her housed and secure next month, next year, next decade. She's never been able to paint her kitchen bright yellow on the spur of the moment just because she felt like it, or faced the fact that if the sticking closet door is going to get fixed, she herself will have to fix it. She doesn't know how hard it is to keep on making the bed and cooking good meals without the spur of someone else's company or approval, nor does she understand the private pleasure of being able to stay up all night reading without worrying about keeping someone else awake.

When my grandmother married, at twenty-two, she went directly from her father's house to her husband's house. The joys of her life haven't included either a home or a room of her own. Her life mirrors the life patterns of my entire family. The only unmarried adult relatives I remember from childhood are my great-aunt Petey, a widow; my great-aunt Lilly, a Benedictine nun; my great-uncle Ron, a gentle and melancholy epileptic; and my uncle Bill, who was divorced under mysterious and scandalous circumstances. These were not, in current parlance, positive role models for independent living. Nor were they people who inspired me to see living alone as an interesting choice rather than a cruel trick of circumstance.

My grandmother is typical not just of our family but of the norms of the polyglot European community from which we sprung. Though there have always been sizable numbers of unmarried people, in historical terms independent single-person households have been rare. People shared dwellings, in groups that included parents and children, half brothers and sisters, servants, wards, retainers, and employees. When Englishman Gregory King drew up a list of typical household sizes in 1688, he estimated that temporal lords such as princes had households of forty people; spiritual lords such as bishops, of twenty; gentlemen, of eight; and "freeholders of the lesser sort," of six. Even "vagrants: as gypsies, thieves, beggars, &c."—that is, the homeless, the disenfranchised—had, according to King, three and a half people per household. No category of being, however marginal, had a household of only one. People who lived alone were odd enough to be frightening, particularly if they were women. Beatrice Gottlieb, the historian who reproduces Gregory King's chart, notes that women who lived alone, without a man's protection, were likely targets for witchcraft persecution. It was easier to believe that a woman was attached to the devil than that she wasn't attached at all. "Anyone who wanted a place in society on any level had to locate herself or himself in a household," Gottlieb writes.

Only in the last century or so have one-person households finally stopped being remarkable and the chance to live alone, at least for a while, come to seem a desirable goal. This is a fruit of urbanization, which made apartment housing and hence smaller living units practical, and of industrialization, which separated the home from the workplace. The change is too recent to be quite incorporated into our collective consciousness, and it happened later for women than for men. Born right at the turn of the century, my grandmother grew up amid this silent social revolution. In the world that shaped her, women were almost always dependent on someone, a father or brother if not a husband. Marriage still marked an economic, sexual, and symbolic passage into adulthood, into even a small measure of independence, into one's full privileges and powers. For the average woman, to be left "on the shelf," as the old phrase had it—unselected, unmarried, looked at but left over—was still a prospect of dependence and restriction. It's no wonder that my grandmother sees in its contemporary equivalent little to celebrate.

I understand all this, but I remain covetous of those plates. More precisely, I covet the recognition, the visibility, they offer. I want my grandmother to see me as I see myself. To value and celebrate my life in its thoughtful and complex choices. To reward me for my independence and to comfort me in my uncertainties and fears. To acknowledge that though my opportunities and choices have been different from hers, I am very much a part of her tradition—that I'm even a homemaker, in my own fashion. It's as natural as it is illogical, this longing to have the matriarch of my tribe give me this emblematic gift, this symbolic blessing. It's also an evasion, and an ironic one—since one of the things that living alone demands of you is that you learn to bless yourself.

❧ ❧

For the past sixteen years, since I left my parents' home, I've always—at least officially—lived alone. For my first apartment I chose a tiny but private studio rather than the larger place I could have afforded with a roommate. I held on to my apartment even during the years when I spent most of my time and left most of my possessions at the home of a lover. I kept the furniture in my empty apartment dusted, the rent and utility bills paid, the refrigerator stocked. I've returned here again and again over the years: for a few days when I needed to concentrate on a deadline or nurse an annoying cough or think through a quarrel, for months or years when a relationship foundered or ended. Over time I've come to love the peaceful setting my apartment offers for my work. I'm more confident about the richness of the life I can achieve from its home base, and less certain that love is necessarily improved by cohabitation. The result of all this is to make me feel increasingly settled in the routine of living alone.

Five or ten years ago, I still thought that the fact that I lived alone was a random chance—a by-product, say, of proposals that came at the wrong time or from the wrong man. Lately I've realized that this isn't entirely true. In theory I find the idea of living with someone at some time interesting, but in practice it's never this interest that actually drives me. Given the choice between the imperfections of a potential spouse or roommate and the imperfections of living alone, I've chosen solitude with a fierce if unconscious consistency.

This has something to do with both taste and habit, but more to do with fear. I know this seems illogical. Many (perhaps most) people find the idea of living alone, particularly as one ages, a terrifying prospect. I'm not immune to such fears. No matter how loving or loved I may be, by living alone I forsake that built-in someone who will call 911 if I get sick suddenly, dispose of the mouse that died under the radiator last night, lend a protective presence when a burglar jimmies the bathroom window open, pay the gas bill if I lose my job, and tell me whether the back of my black skirt needs pressing. It's scary to let go of the solace of—as it were—semi-automatic companionship from someone who *must* put up with me, who is there by default, who need not be called or courted. When crises threaten—when I'm ill or particularly tired or feeling some failure of confidence and nerve—my vulnerability feels like no small weight, no little matter.

But I find a kind of paradoxical safety, a peacefulness, a fundamental rightness in living alone. It is a state of existence that offers no illusions, makes no false promises. There *is* no automatic companionship, the act of living alone tells you, and if there is an inevitability in life, it's that of loss and not connection. Living alone makes no pretense that the separate, shifting islands of human experience can be permanently bridged. It's a gentle reminder that someone else's soul is never your own territory and that passages between the two, being tenuous sometimes to the point of evanescence, should be celebrated rather than taken for granted. In this sense living alone is, for me, an acknowledgment of the existential bottom line.

Living alone offers lots of positive pleasures, but the comfort I take in it is at heart defensive, a strategy based on what feels like the overwhelming likelihood of loss. The smaller deprivations and insecurities it involves seem to me like the early moves of a difficult chess game. I sacrifice my pawns willingly, in the hope of staving off a larger and more devastating defeat.

My wariness is that of someone for whom home is a profound and essential extension of self. I know lots of people for whom such symbolism has no compelling meaning. They may love their dwellings, but for them emotional risk is a function of relationship rather than location. I envy this belief, but I don't share it. For me the risk of losing someone deeply loved is—just—bearable; the risk of losing the harmony and safety and control of my home at the same time is not. I've been open to, even reckless with, relationships, but I've never invited my recklessness home. In the complicated working through of the equation of my life I have always kept my home as the constant: the thing that does not change, the citadel-rock that stays dry even in a tidal wave, the sanctuary that cannot be breached.

To acknowledge the symbolic meaning I attach to living alone has also been to start letting it go—to admit that symbol is not reality, that my dwelling is not in fact my soul, that boundaries and havens can be built of materials less tangible than lathe or plaster. I've found it easier, recently, to imagine myself enjoying without undue panic the adventure of a shared domestic life. But the conjugal living arrangements I'm drawn to remain unconventionally cautious and eccentric ones. A year or so ago, I read a newspaper profile of the writer Margaret Drabble, which mentioned that Drabble and her husband, also a writer, live permanently in two separate London houses. *Costly and inconvenient*, my mind scolded. *Heaven*, my gut replied.

Once I realized that I had repeatedly chosen to live alone, however unconsciously, I began to find the experience interesting in a new way. It became worthy of observation, of attention: not the mere side effect of other decisions but an experience central to the narrative of my life. I was looking a lot at paintings by Degas when I started thinking about this, and it struck me that looking at the work of this notorious semirecluse is something like living alone. The pictures look truncated and unfocused at first. But acknowledge that the placement of the frame only looks haphazard—that the emptinesses and odd croppings are in fact intentional—and you begin to yield to a new and unexpected beauty. The dramas obviously taking place offstage begin to echo and intrigue. The just-glimpsed or partial figures come unpredictably alive. The absences fill with meaning, becoming in themselves a form of abundance. You feel the electric jolt of something new.

Once I understood it to be in some way intentional, once I stopped comparing it to the traditional symmetries and began to observe it for what it is, living alone began to take on a kind of plenitude. It became a positive presence, different but no less real than the actual presence of another human being in my home.

It struck me that it's interesting not dramatic, maybe, but interesting—to come home from an evening with people to the silence of a still apartment. To be surprised, after a day when the solitude of the apartment seems full of comfort, by a night when its stillness feels dry, depriving, and oppressive. (In an autobiography the poet May Sarton quotes a letter from a woman friend who, like Sarton, lives alone: "My experience of great solitude is that its character is unstable—at times exalts and fortifies then soon beats down, and throws one into a starving and thirsty state.") It's interesting to discover what my natural schedule is when there is no one to adapt to or impress. To have to think consciously about when and how I want company. To be asked to attend to the satisfaction of my own hungers, the remedy of my own discomforts. Interesting, even, to have to fix the broken closet door or dispose of that dead mouse under the radiator. Something memorable happens in those struggles with the necessities and the limitations of myself.

The word "interesting" sounds flatter than I mean it to. What I mean is: startling, useful, powerfully if subtly full of the remarkable. Living alone is a school that yields no neat maxims, no simple pieties. It teaches, simply, the habit of intense engagement with one's own consciousness and a willingness to pay attention to the thing at hand. Both are adventurous lessons.

❧

Our culture associates domesticity with conjugality (and with heterosexual, legally sanctioned conjugality, though that's another story). Couples begin their married life with shower gifts, engagement gifts, and wedding gifts. Mostly these presents are objects necessary to domestic life: toasters and table linens, clocks, crystal vases. Now that the traditions of barn raisings and housewarmings have died out, the rituals that go with these gifts are the only major occasions in which our communities participate in the fitting up of a new household.

From a practical standpoint, our unintentional conflation of these two ideas—domestic life and marriage—is humorous more often than it's tragic. I remember a friend, who at thirty-eight was to marry a man of forty-seven, looking at her wedding gifts with mingled amusement and alarm. The gifts were piled on the floor of her apartment, the same place in which she had been living with her beloved for three years and by herself for four years before that: a place amply, even generously, stocked with domestic contrivances and comforts. "So, tell me," she said helplessly, gesturing at the three toaster ovens, "does my family think I had to wait for a marriage license before I could start making toast?" The convention of weddings, of course, would answer yes.

People who live alone lose more through this tradition than matching linens or silver-plated salad servers. The real power of rites like weddings is the fact that they signal and solemnize points of change. They mark the transition to a new state of life dramatically enough to make us pay attention to it, and they affirm that the new manner of living is worthy of care, of investment, of dignity, even of splendor. Like the handing over of gold-plated keys to a city, they signify that one has earned citizenship in a new and exciting world. Like the ritual breaking of a champagne bottle across the bow of a ship, they mark the beginning of a journey.

Inhabiting our homes without such ceremonial lifts over the threshold, those of us who live alone sometimes fail to recognize that home life is—in and of itself, with or without a partner—an enterprise intended to solace, to comfort, to pleasure the body and the soul. With no oversized keys to the domestic city in hand, it's not surprising when we fail to enjoy the full privileges and pleasures of the realm. With no cutting of ribbons or burst of champagne to send us off, we sometimes find ourselves foundering or, worse, still bobbing at dockside long after a voyage should have begun. With no companion to help us position the frame and balance the composition, it's harder to give the experience of domestic life the attention necessary to appreciate the richness of the pattern, the unexpected rightness of its shape.

❦ ❧

I came home from Florida two weeks ago, and I felt again the shock of change. My family's houses had been filled with noise, activity, negotiation, and sometimes the ominous silences of misunderstanding. Going from that unpredictable liveliness into the controlled peace of my apartment was like turning the corner from Broadway onto a peaceful rural lane. One is an experience of quiet and small surprises. The other is variable and startling; it crackles with echo, argument, momentary blare, and vivid pauses.

The picture that hangs higher on the wall than my father likes it, but not quite as high as my mother prefers. My grandfather's bellowed command that my grandmother bring him his glasses, and the quick, half-affectionate, half-exasperated grimace with which she's been fetching them for seventy-five years. The low, strained murmur of my brother's voice as he tries to keep his ebullient sons quiet while their mother marks her second-graders' tests upstairs. The antique candlesticks my sister's husband bought her, and the tacky velour chair he insists on keeping despite her protests, and their daughter's Barbie doll lying naked and abandoned underneath a kitchen chair. My apartment greeted me with no such emblems of compromise, resistance, response. I missed all this liveliness a little, and at the same time savored the sense of coming home to my own haven, my own right place.

On my way to the market to restock my refrigerator I walked past an antique-shop window full of old china. I wandered into the shop to browse, but I walked out with a set of four blue-and-white porcelain dinner plates, affordable only because two of the rims are chipped. I hung the plates on my kitchen wall, on wire hangers that let them go easily when I take them down for use. Someone watching me cook would see them curving over me the same way the Haviland plates halo my grandmother's head at our afternoon teas.

I used the plates last night when I had some friends to dinner. There are no formal settings, no ritual places at my house. There isn't even a real dining table (since I write more than I entertain, I've co-opted it to serve as a desk). I dish out food in the kitchen, and depending on the complexity of the meal, guests put their plates on the coffee table or sit on the floor. It's not ideal, but it works, and I've grown to like the way we all move around, group and regroup as we find the right perches for ourselves. Last night's guests seemed content enough, and the blue-and-white plates looked festive with my deep yellow napkins and the cornflowers I put in a white pitcher my mother gave me for no particular reason last fall.

It didn't occur to me until I was cleaning up afterward

that my new plates were a kind of response to my grand-mother's equivocal not-quite-present. My plates bear no direct resemblance to hers: my unconscious impulse was aimed at giving myself a gift, not at the futile task of replacing what she could give me. Like hers, my plates are good china, but they're English rather than French, blue rather than pink, transfer printed rather than handpainted, eccentrically Gothic rather than serenely classical. The center of each plate, wreathed by an intricate border of blue tracery, is painted with a small landscape, different on each plate though based on the same formula. In the foreground, among rocks and feathery trees, is a woman bedecked in full skirt, parasol, and hat. She may be standing, sitting, or resting against a boulder, but her back is always to the viewer and she is always looking at an exotic scene: a ruined temple ringed by mountains, on one plate; a vaguely ecclesiastical edifice on another; something that looks like the Brighton Pavilion on a third. It was these images that drew me to the plates. There seemed something right, something fitting, about having my dinner on this china: upon these quiet, dreamy pictures of solitary women in mysterious landscapes, marveling at the chasms and enclosures of the world.

Children's Room

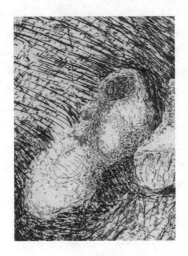

I don't have children, and I doubt I ever will. The reasons

for my childlessness are complicated; circumstance, timing,

the pressure of other dreams, and a simple lack of an overwhelming desire for kids all play a part in it, and so probably does my self-doubt. I'm free of the deep ambivalence about this issue that seems to strike some women at forty—the sudden fear, as time runs out, that they have made the wrong decision. I feel easy and peaceful with my choice. Inevitably, though, given the centrality of this question in a woman's life, I am aware of the absence, and surprise myself sometimes by the way it manifests itself in my consciousness. On sleepless nights, I sometimes find myself remembering the feeling of holding an infant niece or nephew in my arms, nuzzling that trusting heat and weight, smelling the powdery, milky scent. I watch mother-child interactions in the subway or street intently, as if they somehow matter to me. I'll scrutinize books on the decoration of children's rooms carefully, often mentally redesigning the pictures to better shelter a child I'll never have.

I even have a file of shelter magazine clippings about children's rooms. The other day, sorting through it, I came across an article I had torn from the July 1985 issue of *House and Garden* and then forgotten. The piece is about what its writer called the "art-encrusted loft" of the artist Julian Schnabel. It's a standard decorating-magazine production: a handful of big, glossy, gorgeously styled photographs accompanied by a brief and fulsome text. Less typically, it includes a photograph of the Schnabel children's room. Children's rooms aren't usually illustrated in the high-end shelter magazines, though pictures abound of other private spaces, bedrooms, and even baths.

The children's room had "little light," and the Schnabels commissioned an artist to paint trompe l'oeil "sunlight on the walls in murals copied almost exactly from Pompeiian frescoes." *House and Garden*'s picture displays a stretch of pomegranate red wall decorated with faux pilasters, a cartouche of the Three Graces, and around the cornice, a landscape of windblown trees. In an alcove, a single metal camp-style bed sits under a faux mosaic of marigold, ivory, terra-cotta, and warm indigo squares. All of the paint is carefully distressed; it looks old, damaged, decayed. On the grey carpeting in front of the bed rests a gilded Corinthian capital, on the capital an inflatable ball patterned like a globe. The only signs that children inhabit the room are a pair of small dolls on the bed and a bright yellow Sesame Street truck in one corner, backed up against the wall. A trio of balloons is scattered on the floor, but they seem too gorgeously old and fragile to be childlike: they have the umbered hues and softened patina of old Roman glass.

I felt indifferent to the design of the Schnabels' adult rooms. I didn't much like them, but I didn't much care. I did care about that children's room. I didn't like it, and it made me angry. Walls re-creating a town where people died in agony, beds suitable for the itinerant destructiveness of war—the choice of motifs seemed almost hostile. I had a vague sense that the Schnabels' freedom to encrust their loft with postmodern decadence stopped at the children's door, that they had no right to foist their exquisitely self-conscious, gloomily millennial vision on their kids. It was outrage that made me clip the article and put it away, for no particular purpose but that it seemed ineffably wrong.

What strikes me now is how differently I judged those two domains, the one made by adults for adults and the other by adults for children. I applied aesthetic standards to the first and what I can only, reluctantly, call moral standards to the second. Some instinct in me, unknown and unconsidered until then, labeled decorating for adults a pleasure and decorating for kids a responsibility. For a minute I'd felt as sorry for those privileged children as if they'd been deprived of something vital—food, warmth, parental understanding.

As an artist and a successful one, Mr. Schnabel might be expected to have an unusually intense response to interior decoration. When I looked at some books on decorating children's rooms in search of more typical examples, though, I was surprised to see that he wasn't as extreme as I'd thought.

Nursery Style, a 1991 book by Annie Sloan and Felicity Bryan, tells parents how to decorate their children's rooms in various period styles. "The exciting use of stencils for walls, furniture and bed cover, the simple prints, the hooked rugs, carved ornaments, primitive paintings and, above all, the marvelous patchwork and applique quilts and cushions make this a delightful and extremely practical style for a child," says the chapter titled "American Country Style." In her 1992 book *Cradle and All*, Pamela Scurry, owner of two Manhattan shops, writes of the nursery that "the decoration and furnishings should suit the baby's needs and the parents' sense of style . . . the modern nursery is a child's own magic realm." Like Sloan and Bryan, she finds some of this magic in the reconstitution of the past. Also like them, she divides things up by gender. One caption notes that "Victorian silver pieces can be transformed into containers for cotton balls and cotton swabs. The traditional canopy of the antique hanging cradle resembles a bridal veil, with Alençon lace and a circle of silk flowers at the crown."

These books are aimed at parents wealthy enough to invest considerable money in their children's rooms and sophisticated enough to appreciate historical references. The 1987 edition of *The Better Homes and Gardens Book of Interior Design*, created for a less rarified, middle-class audience, echoes the same ideas more modestly. "A child's room should be a very personal place—a special little world," it says. "Think back to when you were a child. Chances are, you craved a canopy bed," a caption notes. "This four-poster canopy was passed down from mother to daughter. The same is true for the handsome old highboy. . . . A prim print wall covering in soft cornflower blue and white stripes adds to the yesteryear appeal."

Small recreations of an idealized nineteenth-century past are less offensive than the Schnabels' reprise of Pompeii. At least they're metaphors of safety, of history inherited rather than lost. But like the Schnabels' room, almost all of them advance, through everything from rugs to lamp shades, a single theme, a vision: of the classical past or the prim innocence of girlhood, of American simplicity or preindustrially simple English life. Almost all of them are young children's spaces, as though the interest inherent in a child's room ends once the child is old enough to know his or her own mind. Almost all of them are elaborately styled. Few—if any—of them respond to a specific child's tastes or quirks.

When I first began looking at rooms like these, they made me uneasy. They reminded me of commercial valentines, which pay homage not to a beloved so much as to the idea of love. In their complex confections, the human particularity of the beloved—the quirkiness, contradictions, and changeability—is subsumed into a grander vision, an unchanging, undying ideal. The adult in me distrusts this generality and sentimentality, and found it easy to deride the sometimes silly elaboration of the rooms. The child in me saw a different truth. At five, or eight, or even eleven, I would have loved to have one of the rooms Scurry, Bryan, or Sloan pictures. I would have felt special amid the Victorian frills; I would have adored a canopy bed.

❧

Our culture envisions childhood as a state like no other: magical, innocent, loving; dreamy and energetic; vulnerable but also powerful, with a vision unfettered by the conventions that shackle the adult mind. In some ways, in fact, we view childhood the way the Victorians did woman- or maidenhood: as a sacred and fragile state to which we owe our greatest veneration, our most meticulous care. I don't mean to deny the real vulnerability of children or denigrate our concern for them through this comparison with an ideal that (in Western cultures at least) has largely passed away. I only want to suggest that like all ideals, this one is highly charged with hope and fear, founded as much on unconscious anxieties as on the complexities and observations of particular human lives.

We take the importance and value of childhood so much for granted that it's difficult to comprehend how recent an idea this is. Through most of European history, people with children worried not about failures of nurturing but, as the historian of childhood Philippe Ariès says, about "the honour of the line, the integrity of an inheritance, or the age and permanence of a name"—questions of prestige and property. They were concerned with the House, not the home. The emotional ideal of the home we take for granted today—that crucial soft nest for the fragile young, place of private and almost hermetic bonding, nexus of affections born from and relying on a conjugal bond, beloved and necessary retreat—didn't begin to arise until the seventeenth century.

Until it did, family emphasis was on the performance of standard roles—the just father, the obedient child—and on the preparation necessary to fit the child into his or her eventual place in the family's economic and social life. The idea that childhood was somehow magical, or that children needed a private place to dream or retreat, would have been greeted with bafflement, if not derision. Like adults, even wealthy children in earlier centuries shared spaces: they slept with servants, other children, their nurses, their parents. Why remove a child from the pleasure and information to be gained from the social life of the house? Why answer in the child a need that even adults were not thought to have?

In the seventeenth and eighteenth centuries, the idea of childhood changed gradually but dramatically, part of a radical redefinition of the shape of society and the value and prerogatives of the self. For the first time, private life was accorded a value of its own. Ideals of affectionate, equally apportioned, and hands-on parenting; of family bonds that come from personal affection rather than standard roles; of the pleasures of intimacy and privacy, all began to develop. With them, childhood ceased to seem merely a prelude to adulthood and began to become what it is today, the conceptual center of the family home. By the turn of the nineteenth century, Blake and Wordsworth were waxing lyrical about a childhood not just different from but superior to maturity, an idyllic, visionary state.

Actual children's rooms took a long time to catch up with changing perceptions. Wealthy and even prosperous nineteenth-century families did have nurseries (the poor, then as earlier, lived too closely together for such luxuries), but references to them illustrate and describe spare or even bleak spaces. A not atypical 1853 watercolor of the nursery at one of the German palaces depicts a small princeling and his rocking horse looking lost in a vast, formal room decorated entirely with adult-scale furniture in what was by then the very outdated Empire style. Some of this bleakness is explained by the fact that the nineteenth-century nursery was still a place of adult instruction rather than childish retreat. The nursery-

and-schoolroom suite housed not only children but nannies, governesses, and tutors; it was a workplace, for these professionals as well as for the children themselves. Not until the educational process was moved out of the home was the child's room free to become the dreamy private retreat we know today, a place designed for respite rather than effort.

Looking at this history has an oddly reassuring effect: what strikes me, immediately, is how various the approaches to child raising have been and how resiliently children, at least as a group, have survived them. Seen from a historical perspective, the modern ideal of childhood looks relatively benign, if a little grandiose. So do modern children's rooms. Their overt display of cost and status, however distasteful, is actually no more blatant than the displays of family pomp and power taken for granted for centuries. Their attempts to create a kind of dream vision are sometimes sentimental, but still preferable to a home in which there is no place for youthful quietude or retreat. Their excesses, though sometimes bizarre, nevertheless seem preferable to an aesthetic of chill isolation and didacticism. At worst, like those store-bought valentines, modern children's rooms—like modern parents—may simply try too hard.

My own parents gave little organized attention to the question of decorating for children. They decorated the nursery and later the room I shared with my twin brother cheerfully but simply and inexpensively. By the time I was nine, they had begun to give me some control. I wanted Beatles wallpaper that year. My mother tried to talk me out of it, but after almost a year of my desperate pleading, my parents gave in. A double roll of John, Paul, George, and Ringo appeared under the Christmas tree. I was ecstatic. It wasn't very attractive or well made wallpaper, and it didn't create the kind of special room I craved. I outgrew it quickly. My parents made me live with it awhile, giving me a valuable early lesson about the danger of decorating fads.

The year I turned thirteen, my parents built a new master bedroom and I, inheriting their old space, got my own room for the first time. I redecorated immediately. My parents helped me paint the room—an intense lavender, not the royal purple I wanted but as close as my conservative father would permit—and let me pick out a rug, an inexpensive purple shag. Baby-sitting earnings paid for cheap purple drapes, purple-and-turquoise quilted bedspreads, and a battered Salvation Army bureau that I enameled a glossy and unnatural aqua. My father built shelving, which I painted purple and arranged with peacock feathers, peace symbols, scented candles shaped like mushrooms, and crystal unicorns. One wall of the room was covered by a vast corkboard, and on that crumbling sandwich board of the soul I pinned Beardsley posters, newspaper clippings, pictures of Winnie-the-Pooh and Mick Jagger, reproductions of Degas ballerinas, and a series of quotations from what might be called the Meaningfully Vague school of literature, from Kahlil Gibran to Carole King. I loved that room, and it is much to my parents' credit that I thought they loved it, too.

Like sensible rulers of modern monarchical states, they had relinquished much of their power over my small territory gracefully, rather than wait for me to wrest it from them. The role they played within its boundaries was largely ceremonial. They arrived to utter words of encouragement, made occasional, apparently casual inspections, and exerted just enough pressure to reassure me. Their periodic injunctions to *clean up that room, damn it*, were proof that my life was still under a comfortably nominal control.

My mother and father kept their own taste, their concerns about appropriateness and status, out of my room. If they needed to express their creativity or prove that they were good parents, they did so beyond my door. Thanks to their restraint, my room served me exactly as I needed it to, as both laboratory and experiment, both stage and stand-in. Outside of it I was paralyzed by limitations, real and imagined. I was too cautious, too sensible, too *good* a girl to act out my tenuous independence through drink, drugs, sex, or even hanging out late at the local Friendly's. I was too self-conscious to express my fantasies or fears in art (I dabbled energetically in the less revealing crafts of jewelry making and leaded glass instead). I was too skinny and bespectacled to rebel through dress, though the era encouraged outrageous female costumings. My room gave me my only intimations of the delights of autonomy and excess. It wasn't a fantasy, it was *all* fantasies—as ambitious and undecided as I was. Sitting in its purple shadows, breathing in its perfumed fin de siècle air, listening to the theatrical austerity of Gregorian chant or the theatrical anarchy of the Rolling Stones, I felt myself a creature of infinite possibility, a future Grace Slick, a future Gloria Steinem, or both at once.

My old purple room is gone. By now, maybe, it's once again a master bedroom. Or maybe it's a girl's room still: with posters of punk rockers, or frills and a pale pink rug. Someone else's daughter, someone else's dream. But every time I move someplace new, I pull my beloved purple room out of mental storage. Back then I savored my chance to try out adult powers within the still-secure world of the child. Now I struggle against the inevitable limitations of my adult homes with a measure of the child's transformative glee. By not decorating my room too well, by letting me struggle with it, my parents gave me the confidence that with a little help, I could make something out of nothing by myself. In this respect, the most important thing they gave me was their own detachment, their own restraint.

My parents, like many others, had a difficult time staying afloat in the white water of their daughter's impending adulthood, but they navigated this particular shoal with skill. I would have preferred the ready-made glamour of department-store Victorian then, but I'm grateful now. They didn't give me Eden, as the parents in the books I quoted earlier seem to want to do. They didn't see that as their job. They let me learn that I could make Eden, or Edens, for myself. That is an inestimably greater, maybe more difficult, and certainly more necessary gift.

Entrance Hall Two

I've just finished redecorating the front hallway of my

apartment, a project that has left me feeling festive and self-

congratulatory. Windowless, narrow, and taller than it is

long, the hall will never be graceful, but my efforts have given it a little charm. I'm pleased by the fresh white gleam of the doors, the ornate scrollings of the small brass chandelier, the tautness of the chintz I stretched and stapled onto the walls and ceiling. With its dense thicket of flowers so precisely rendered and so improbably combined, the fabric reminds me of the aster-and-zinnia-filled gardens I helped plant as a child: a magical result, given the modesty of the means. I'm still enjoying the surprise of opening my front door onto flowers rather than the plain taupe paint I chose four years ago in a less effervescent mood. This time, I tell myself as I put away my paintbrushes and staple gun, I've found the perfect solution to this imperfect space: more welcoming than that depressing taupe, more unusual than the striped wallpaper before that, more practical than the ivory or pale yellow gloss of still earlier redecorations.

Scratch any wall of my small apartment and you'll find the same layers of color and pattern, the same cycle of hope, disappointment, and revision. I count my twelve years here not by jobs gained, lovers lost, or essays written, but by floors refinished and rooms redone. That, I think, was the year I retiled the kitchen; that was the year I built the shelves above the desk. This project will be easy, I say, consigning myself to yet another Saturday of effort. As rapidly as a season or a seedling, the apartment evolves. Infrequent visitors are startled to find the rooms they remember gone, replaced by colors and moods entirely new. "Am I crazy, or did this room used to be blue-and-white?" one asked recently, baffled, sitting among cabbage-rose-printed pillows on a mossy green sofa. The blue-and-white toile slipcovers he remembered are folded in the closet, along with the lace curtains and architectural prints that went with them, part of the hoard of raw materials waiting to be recombined once again.

All this refurbishing sounds—is—obsessive. But what I was aware of, just finished with my hallway, was not its compulsiveness but its abundance, its sensuality. Standing on my ladder and shaking loose the lengths of the hallway's chintz, which billowed out as glowing and sumptuous as the swags in a Baroque portrait, I felt as though I were raising a symbolic flag affirming the generous over the meager, the vivid over the drab, the extravagant over the sensible. Brushing the snowy paint over its dull ground in broad, cleansing swaths, I experienced for a moment the forgiving mutability of things, the grace with which the old order sometimes can give way to the new. Even the work itself—the stretching and stapling and brushing—was satisfying, more like gardening, say, than housework: instructive, tangibly productive, and utterly relaxing.

I inherited the knack and habit of redecoration from my father. This unintentional legacy is as much a part of my home as the actual gifts he's given me, the things he's fixed or helped me buy. In 1958, when I was three, my parents bought the kind of residence euphemistically known as a "fixer-upper," a big old stucco house made affordable by the corrosion of its pipes, the buckling of its floorboards, and the abundance of old tires and scrap metal growing on its lawn.

For the next twenty-nine years, the family would spend most of its weekends salvaging this noble wreck.

My brother and sister and I fetched tools, steadied ladders, swept up grass cuttings, and waited to be of use, as silent and compliant as acolytes. My mother helped with the more technical tasks, stood ready with sandwiches for lunch breaks postponed until late afternoon, and made emergency raids on Schantz's Hardware, where she searched through the dusty bins for just the right washer, window catch, pipe elbow, or tile grout.

It was my father who made the schedule, defined the agenda, and set the tone of those working weekends. He is the child of resolutely undomestic parents, second-generation Austrian immigrants who, once they became successful, made every effort to leave the traditional, home-centered life of the old country behind. By the time I knew Molly and Leo, they lived in a penthouse in Palm Beach, a bright glossy place full of imitation Louis XIV furniture; when we visited they would show us clippings from the newspaper social pages, pictures of themselves holding bridge-competition blue ribbons or stepping out of expensive restaurants. Brought up in apartments, taken care of by baby-sitters and maids, my father once told me that the single home-maintenance task he had learned as a child was how to call the super.

Without confidence or skill or the money to hire experts, my father faced home ownership with what must certainly have been, at least at first, anxiety, if not outright terror. He wanted almost obsessively to do right by his house, his family, his commitments. He threw himself into maintaining the house with the kind of rigid excess sometimes seen in religious converts, an overcompensation marked by fervent study, constant attention, and scrupulous adherence to even the finest points of the rules.

Under his tense but energetic stewardship, the broken bones of the house reknit themselves. Over the years, the pipes burst and the cellar flooded more rarely; gradually our projects moved from the realm of repair into that of refurbishment. My father built a greenhouse, refinished Victorian furniture that neighbors had thrown away, retiled the kitchen, and planted the stiff, colorful gardens of which my hallway fabric reminds me. Conscious of his scrutiny, I became deft with trowel, paintbrush, and tack hammer, but I remained, like my brother and sister, merely an assistant, and despite the decreasing urgency of the tasks, the family energies remained consecrated to work instead of leisure. I grew to resent this unceasing round of labor, the unstated demand that I present myself each weekend as a kind of ritual sacrifice on the altar of family cooperation and respectable home ownership. Still, the family ethic rooted itself invisibly in me. It would take years for me to comprehend how precisely, how unconsciously, I had copied my own domestic life on this model, or with what unquestioning energy I measured myself against the dogged perfectionism of my father.

The flowers of my new hallway spring from this mixed soil. Those childhood weekends gave me the skill and knowledge I needed to handle the work of redoing the hall and the confidence I needed to start the job in the first place. But they gave me, too, a punishing awareness of every imperfection, every inadequacy in my work. Now that the hallway is finished, I'm troubled by the ripples near the edge of the closet door, the slight unevenness in the paint of the linen cupboard. I have to force my attention away from the fact that the seams of the ceiling were hastily done, that I never did get around to finishing off the baseboards with the matching cord I meant to buy. These minor flaws, barely noticeable to anyone else, feel to me not only visible but significant, as though they were signs of carelessness, laziness, some fundamental flaw of character.

Eventually, if history repeats itself, it will occur to me that my bright hallway lacks a certain sophistication, or elegance, or a suitably postmodern sense of irony. I'll begin to notice more interesting possibilities as I leaf through decorating magazines: a neat striped wallpaper here, a faux stonework finish there, a gorgeous pomegranate-hued paint somewhere else. It will begin to seem reasonable, even commendable, to improve this space once more. My wonderful floral chintz will risk becoming nothing more than the next-but-last layer of the hallway, long before it is worn or even outdated.

This is the other face of my personal Janus-god of redecoration: a face hostile rather than benign, grudging instead of generous. The voice that issues from it insists that nothing is ever pretty enough, good enough, finished enough. That at the heart of existence is something that must be repaired.

That every impression must be rehearsed and rehearsed again. That virtue is a matter not of understanding or experience, but of unceasing effort, and that the perfection attained by the detail is more important than the pleasure afforded by the whole. At its worst, this internal voice makes me restless and uneasy in the same space I've tried so hard to make relaxing. A friend who came to dinner recently commented on how much she liked my apartment. Where she saw abundance—of warmth, color, ingenuity, care—it was all too easy for me to see absence: the floorboards I missed, the valances I haven't yet sewn, the lamp shade that needs replacing. Ironically, I'm more at home in her casual, untidy apartment—hastily painted by the tenant before her and unapologetically furnished with cast-offs—than I am in my own. Her place looks less Edenic than mine, but there seems to be no subtle, dangerous serpent hiding among the leaves.

Five years ago, my parents abruptly sold our family home and bought a brand-new house in Florida. I had long been living on my own, but the news shook me. For better or worse I loved our house. It had shaped me. I had defined myself in resistance and in submission to it. I grieved at its loss. And I felt angrily confused at seeing my father abandon the object of so much labor and attention—not only his, but mine. It felt like a betrayal of family closeness and continuity, and also of the values—the harsh perfectionism as well as the love of domestic work—he had instilled in me. Helpless to comprehend, I wondered if my parents were simply getting too old to cope.

I still didn't understand when I made my first visit to Florida, three months later. My parents' new house was neat, pretty, and compact, devoid of both the character and the flaws of the old one. The window frames, the door latches, the professionally papered walls, the immaculate carpeting, even the coil of pipes visible below the kitchen sink, all had a shining perfection. The house was a comfortable and easy place, but it didn't match either my notion of a home or my notion of the home my father would choose. "Don't you miss our house? Don't you miss having an old house to tinker with?" I asked him. He looked past me, past the window with its perfectly fitting screen, out onto a lawn kept neat by a weekly mowing service. "No," he said confidently. "I don't miss it at all."

In the years since then I have watched my parents' lives blossom—not steadily or quickly, but surely—in this place of respite and leisure. From this perspective the sale of the family house makes more sense. It occurs to me that my parents moved not because they felt old, but because they felt young enough to try to achieve another, less burdened way of living. It has become easier to comprehend why my father so abruptly changed his life—quit cold turkey, as it were—and so completely removed himself from the temptations of renovations and repairs. I'm still optimistic enough, or maybe arrogant enough, to believe that I can change without resorting to such extreme measures. But like him, I've begun to attempt to unlearn those punitive old lessons. I haven't yet managed to silence that insidious inner voice. But, like a veteran who still hears the gunfire of a long-finished war, I am beginning to learn to ignore it. My new hallway isn't safe, but it has at least a fighting chance at survival.

When I visited my parents this summer I noticed that they had made some small changes around the house. The kitchen had been repainted. They had planted a few new rosebushes, bought some new dining room chairs. But if they had more projects in mind, I didn't learn of them. I spent my two weeks there writing a little, reading a little, walking on the beach, watching my father play golf, browsing the antique shops with my mother. I got nothing in particular accomplished, except that I finally felt a little of the protected aimlessness, the pleasantly mild boredom, of the childhood weekends and summers I'd never quite had.

Together, one twilight, the three of us strolled around the backyard, with its dense, fragrant borders of vinca, oleander, hibiscus, and rose. It's a little like a room, this garden, small and private, enclosed within its free-form verdant walls. The weeding, my father said as he gestured toward tufts of crabgrass and self-seeded fern, would have to wait for the cooler days of winter. During the hot months he'd taught himself not to notice. We spent a full hour in the garden that night, and we didn't plan a project or pull a weed. In fact, we didn't improve a single thing.

Guest Room

I had never seen the place before, but I felt immediately at

home. The sturdy rattan chairs, the plump sofa with its loose

ticking-stripe slipcover companionably creased where someone had been sitting, the single blue pottery bowl placed asymmetrically on the mantel seemed right together, unified by the beauty of their materials and the simplicity of their form. The low, elegiac sun of a clear West Coast afternoon gilded the picture frames and the fur of two calico cats who sprawled sleepily near the window, unalarmed by my entrance. The apartment, on the ground floor of a squat Spanish building stuccoed an improbable lobster pink, was larger, lighter, and sparser than my own in New York. But the stacks of art books, the scattering of small photographs and prints, the geraniums on the windowsills were much like mine. I recognized, too, the attention that had been given to their choice and placement, the care lavished on the making of a home.

I had come to Los Angeles to visit my friend Jane, a curator in a city museum. In the fifteen years since our graduation from college, we've shared the kind of deep but undemanding friendship possible, sometimes, between people who see each other only rarely. Until this visit I had seen her only in New York and known her lover, Daniel, only through her words: *editor, intelligent, interested in Eastern philosophy, a good man.* Yes, I thought on meeting him, a good man—vital, sane, humorous. Jane herself, dressed in baggy shorts and a sweater instead of the well-cut dresses she wore in New York, seemed lighthearted, welcoming, and at ease.

After I dropped my bags in the small guest room we ate dinner at a casual Mexican restaurant, got silly on one beer apiece, went to bed early. Over the weekend, Jane and Daniel assembled for me a mosaic of their lives: *This was the exhibition I curated, the best junk shop in town, our favorite street, the fabric I was telling you about—do you think I should make the pillows piped, or fringed?* Together, that day and the next, the three of us performed the unconscious rituals that cement new and deepening bonds: sitting for hours over dinner; laughing over bad puns; standing in the darkened hallway at night, the cats nuzzling drowsily at our ankles, talking again about politics or dictionaries or feminist photographers though we'd already said good night. Small acts, at once silly and significant; affirmations of relief, recognition, delight: *Yes, I feel at home here; it was good that I came.* Friday and Saturday night I slept dreamlessly in the guest room under Daniel's mother's aunt's patchwork quilt, Jane's girlhood copy of *Little Women* abandoned on the spare pillow, the plumper of the cats curled companionably in the crook of my bent knees, the tensions of life in New York put blessedly to rest.

Sunday night I woke abruptly, in terror.

The phosphorescent dial of the bedside clock said twotwenty. The room was dim but not dark, luminous with the odd orange glow of streetlights filtered through Japanese rice paper shades. I squinted fiercely, trying to force my eyes to explain my inexplicable fear. Blurrily, I could see that the door to my room, shut tight at bedtime, was now slightly open. A crack showed through to the blackness of the hallway beyond, like the narrow dark fissure in rock that marks a tremor's damage.

Wide awake now, my mind reached for narratives to knit that crack and my terror back into the fabric of the safe known world. *It's just one of the cats, the settling of the house, Jane or Daniel up for an insomniac's cup of tea; it's just my own New York paranoia.* But my body ignored these stories. To the heart knocking against the cage of my chest like a desperate animal and to my air-starved lungs, they were as irrelevant and distanced as fairy tales. Insistent as this sense of danger was my sense of powerlessness. Without my contact lenses, which sat in useless sterility in the guest bathroom, I could barely see. Rigid with fear, I could barely move. Without information I couldn't decide, couldn't choose among the non-choices: *scream, run, wait, play dead and it will go away.*

From the hall came a sound, less footfall than shuffle, too purposeful for a cat, too furtive for Jane or Daniel. The definitiveness of it steadied me, loosened the paralysis of self-doubt. *Lie still,* I told myself. *He*—odd, how it was so clearly a "he"—*might realize that there are three people in the apartment, tenants upstairs, neighbors next door; might figure out how little good stealable stuff there is; might just give up and go.* I was still hoping when—*too soon, inevitably too soon*—the door opened and he entered the room, a dense tall shape, a blurred pillar, a dark absence in the luminous haze of the night. He was a yard from the bed when I sat up, moved by no conscious intention, and screamed. Loudly, unbelievably loudly, making a noise that bore no resemblance at all to my thin and civilized speaking voice, a sound that came from the gut and not the throat. A cry of relief and release, a denial of denial, a claim of outrage, a demand for succor and awareness. In the retelling, days and weeks after, I would find myself saying to friends that *I screamed so loudly I even scared myself,* and I would find that tired formula to be literally true. To give voice to such abandoned, primal horror was in some way to create it, to usher it from the shadow realm of *This can't be happening* into the glare of *Oh dear God it is.*

Everything accelerated now. He lunged toward me until I could feel his breath—*Does he have a knife, a gun? Is he crazy?*—but having started, I couldn't stop screaming, screams loud enough to be a physical force, screams that must have hit him painfully, palpably, like blows. There was movement from Jane and Daniel's room. The intruder turned abruptly and ran. I could hear his footfalls thudding, loudly now, toward the back of the apartment. Suddenly I was out of bed, Daniel was holding my arms, Jane was dialing 911; suddenly we were huddling in the once-comforting hallway with the lights belatedly on, hearing the idle banging of the kitchen door and a scuffling retreat through the shrubs out back. Time steadied again, and in three minutes that felt once more like minutes two policewomen with cumbersome gun belts and long polished nails were taking names, examining bolts and catches, constructing a narrative of slipped window locks and weekend burglaries, dusting the door handles and windowsills for prints.

Already, my mind began to categorize, to label. *Crime: not violent—unintentionally violent—accidentally violent—violent—horrifically, sickeningly, grotesquely violent. Results: none—*

fear and terror only—some injury—much injury—annihilation.
Among the stores of information I had unconsciously accumulated over the years—the tales of friends of friends, the newspaper stories, the sound bites of the nightly news—was a surfeit of rape, torture, humiliation, death. I knew too much not to feel self-conscious, as if my fear or shock were too loud, too demanding, too unreasonable. *No, nothing really happened. Nothing. When I screamed he ran away. No, nothing at all was taken. No, really, fine, just a little shaken, a little scared.* I began, already, to develop a slightly coy, sheepish manner, an act of self-deprecating humor.

My mind wanted to be fair, unselfish, reasonable; to keep things in perspective; to avoid self-pity or overdramatization. Not so my body. My gut, heart, and stomach—those churning, vital organs, so much less effete and disconnected than the brain—neither craved the carrot of respect nor feared the stick of ridicule. My body knew what it knew. For it, all the categories of *That would have been worse* meant nothing, so rumored were they, so abstract, so patently the product of rationalization, distance, and denial. As I waited for the police to finish their work, my body knotted itself into an elaborate storklike posture, my arms wrapped around my torso, one of my legs twisted unnaturally around the other, my jaw clenched. Instinctive reactions to violation, gestures of defense.

I had assumed that Jane and Daniel's house was safe. So had they. Their house, like mine, seemed full of harmony, integrity, authority—of safety and completeness. Our rooms were worlds of order, small universes under control. The pleasure and ease implicit in them was real; the dangerous illusion came from assuming that they were emblems of the world outside. That their balance or serenity exerted, by osmosis, some soothing force. That sheer prettiness and care drew a line of protection around our houses, as invisibly powerful as a taut electric fence.

I was fooled into believing in this mystical protection partly because I wanted to be. Like so many other inhabitants of our embattled age. I'd found it easier to feel cheated than responsible, more fun to sew cushions than to worry over the merits of movement-sensitive floodlights. I'd felt entitled to a house that would be my castle, safe and inviolate. This was part of my heritage, I'd thought; a given, a right.

No such house exists, and no such house has ever existed. The design of even fairy-tale castles arises from the logistics of defense: moats, drawbridges, crenellations through which arrows can be shot. Cottagers in medieval Europe, always aware of the possibility of theft, simply kept their possessions in chests too cumbersome to steal easily. Those too poor to afford chests of their own sometimes kept their goods—things as poignantly small to our eyes as blocks of candle wax—in locked trunks at their parish churches. Thieves, highwaymen, and burglars were a fact of eighteenth- and nineteenth-century life. That night at Jane and Daniel's, all these history-class facts came back to me in a new and unwelcome way. For the first time, I had to accept the fact that just being in a house had never kept people totally safe and that it almost certainly never would.

After the intrusion Daniel and Jane and I sat together on the slipcovered couch, drinking tea until we fell asleep at dawn. That day, we drove up into the thready, rock-imperiled roads of Topanga Canyon, past the costly houses of Malibu propped, with apparent insecurity, on the eroding face of the cliff. We lay on a blanket on the beach at Point Dume, surrounded by the innocent violence of sunburn and sibling arguments, not quite reading the books we'd brought with us, allowing ourselves to be comforted by the flat uniform light of the shore, the populated expanse of the beach that made no pretense of enclosure.

We were tender with one another, affectionate, solicitous, but the intrusion had changed us and our relations to one another. Jane and Daniel's experience, of waking to the surprise of raucous, defensive screams, had not been the same as my experience, of waking to the responsibility of aggressively quiet footsteps. Suddenly there were things that couldn't be said. I thought, knowing the thought to be irrational, that if I acknowledged my terror I might make them feel guilty or scare Jane, who spent nights alone in the apartment when Daniel traveled. Maybe they thought, in the days that followed, that if they wanted to sleep with their door shut or the living room light off—if they wanted to argue or make love or just go back to life as usual—they were being ungenerous or unsupportive in the face of my obvious fear. All of us felt a formality, a self-consciousness, that we had not felt before.

And in a way the intrusion depersonalized us all, re-duced—or raised—us to primal roles. Suddenly Jane and Daniel were not just my particular friends but also, more simply, hosts who had failed to honor the sacred trust of pro-tecting the guest-friend given shelter. In the same way, I had become the archetypal stranger, the other, the outsider, who had opened the door of the house and let the evil of the out-side in.

Despite our affection and goodwill, the intrusion divided us. Even more powerfully, it left me feeling divided within myself. On Monday night, the night after what the police called "the incident," I fell immediately into the heavy sleep of exhaustion. On Tuesday night, after an hour or so of un-easy drowsing, I woke. I could feel the weariness of my body, its craving for sleep, a dull, heavy need as distinct as hunger or thirst. But I couldn't rest. Hearing the creaks and breath-ings of the house, I sang myself the familiar lullabies I'd used since I began to live, alone, in dangerous cities: *It's nothing, it's probably nothing, of course it's nothing.* But it was no longer nothing, no longer even improbable. It could happen. It *had* happened. Those reassurances were like a muffler so full of holes it could no longer protect me against the cold. I couldn't decide what to do. *Go to sleep. Watch. Stop worrying. Worry.*

I was terrified again, and paralyzed, and worst of all, ashamed. I was sure that there was no one out in the hallway, but I couldn't move, turn on the light, prove to myself that the hall held only the shadows of books, baskets, maybe a restless cat. The fresh simplicity of the guest room could no longer soothe me. I tried to read, but now the pieties of the March girls seemed alienating, belated: a distant island sighted while I was drowning miles away, already thrashing, sinking, lost.

On Friday night I flew back home, to New York. It was hard to leave Jane and Daniel, but I felt relieved to be returning to my own private place. Usually I returned to the city with ambivalence, disliking its greyness, its bars and barbed wire. This time, its defensiveness reassured me. I didn't notice the usual welcoming objects in my own apartment, my desk and my books, the pots of flowers, the small paintings, the photographs of family and friends. Instead I was glad of the things that I had seen, before, as failures or frustrations. The near-claustrophobic smallness of the space, the kitchen and bathroom windows looking over a narrow, impenetrable alley, and the grim locked security gate on the fire escape window now seemed reassuring, signals of enclosure and control.

On the phone that week, Jane and Daniel told me that they had repaired their cut-open screen, screwed in new window locks, forced their landlord to install lights in their backyard. Still, Jane said, when Daniel was away she left the lamps on all night and woke at three in the morning, frightened and edgy. I checked the perimeter of my apartment obsessively before I went to bed, programmed the memory of my phone with 911, kept it at my bedside. Still, I slept badly. It was less painful to be so frightened alone, less embarrassing to lose control when there was no one watching. But the terror itself didn't stop. The early part of the night remained a battle between the part of my mind that said, *There is no one here*, and the part that said, *But there could be. There could be.* Even when exhaustion forced a truce and I fell asleep, my body stayed vigilant. Jerking into awareness every time a pigeon landed on the outside sill or the wind overturned a trash can in the alley. Reading human shape into the shadows of armchairs and lamps every time I woke.

It's been almost a year since that night. Jane and Daniel both found new jobs and moved to New York this May. Their new apartment is smaller, darker, less gorgeously serene than their place out West. Like mine, it has bars on the windows.

My nighttime terrors have diminished, and I've gotten better at handling them. I go places prepared, now, for a flaring up of my fear, which returns each time I spend the night someplace new. I'm better at accepting the fact that some of those nights will feel as extended—as endlessly, nightmarishly dragged out—as the few minutes of vulnerability they pay perverse homage to. I've learned to coddle myself a little, like a frightened child. I don't talk about my fear a lot, but when I do I don't say it's nothing. The most difficult thing to come to terms with, I've realized, isn't the fear. It's the loss of my belief in the great good place, the beautiful fortress. I have fallen from a perch in an ivory tower, where the home is always safe, into a chasm, just as exaggerated, in which it never is. What I hope for my future is a middle ground, less dramatic, more responsive, more particular.

A few months ago, I had a very bad night. In the morning I searched through the boxes in my basement. I found what I was looking for: a porcelain night-light a friend gave me years ago, one of those gifts I keep only out of loyalty. Ornate and sentimental, it's a squat dome of crudely molded china flowers on a fanciful metal stand. It has nothing to do with beauty, or decorative harmony, or taste, and its wedding-cake embellishment looks wrong and disharmonious among my carefully chosen things. Still, I replaced the tiny lightbulb in its base and plugged it in. That night in the dark apartment, it glowed dimly, shedding just enough light to reveal the familiar shapes and comforts of the room. That night my sleep was surer, a little bit less broken. I rested, tenuously and temporarily peaceful, in the fragile patchwork unity of dreams.

Sickroom

The second-to-last time I visited my aunt Jeanne's house,

she had already moved out of it. *Been* moved out of it is more

accurate, actually. Bedridden, dying of breast cancer, she

was unable to pack or walk by herself or even lift her upper body from the tilted white surface of her nursing-home bed.

By then Jeanne's house had already begun to yield up its privacy, making my family more intimate with her weaknesses and secrets than she had ever wanted us to be. By asking us to take care of her in this final illness, Jeanne had tacitly invited us into her home, exposed to us possessions and parts of the house once hidden. My father, who had taken over her finances, had discovered brown paper grocery sacks stuffed with two years of unopened bills, bank statements, dividend checks, tax forms. My mother, who fed and bathed and kept Jeanne company until her hospitalization, had discovered closets crammed to bursting with linens and cabinets stocked with a compulsive's hoard of food. Jeanne's crowded house, with its almost cancerous abundance, belied the capable and imperious face she had presented to the world, revealing a woman less controlled and in greater emotional pain than any of us had known.

By the time I entered Jeanne's house this next-to-last time, some of its possessions were already mine. A year before this visit, already very ill, she had told me that she'd like me to have her late husband's desk, an old wooden armchair, an Arts and Crafts lamp, and a small majolica pitcher. She had not yet died when I made this visit, but she had seen these things for the last time. The desk, lamp, and pitcher did not yet belong to me, but I belonged to them in a way Jeanne no longer did. I still belonged to the world of writing, reading, sitting at a table; to the domain of small domestic pleasures, to the continuity of life.

❧ ❧

When I was a child I believed that Jeanne was the only relative I resembled: that among a clan who did not look or think like me she was my closest match. Like me, she had been the older of two girls, a sister who envied and bossed a more ebullient sibling. Like me, she was thin, dark, studious, artistic. Even her flaws bound me to her, or so I thought. In her shyness, and the weapon she made of her intellect, I thought I saw the precursor of my sarcasm, my lack of charm. When bad things happened to her—a divorce, a problematic son, the first bout of breast cancer—I read them as omens. By the time of her final illness I had half forgotten this mystical sense of linked destinies. Still, some of my identification with her must have lingered on, like the blurred afterimage of things vividly seen that sometimes persists even after you've closed your eyes. The news of her sickness hit home in an urgent, personal way.

For the first time I thought about my apartment in terms of mortality, as a body of intimate information that might be revealed without my consent or control. How would my mother, sister, friend, lover judge the jumbled pile of clothes at the bottom of my extra closet, the gropingly inarticulate drafts of my first poems, the rarely defrosted freezer with its arctic weight of ice? What would my apartment tell them about me that they didn't know and maybe didn't want to? Who would understand the meaning of the eighteenth-century headboard I got at a garage sale, or my mother's opal ring? More practically, how would all of my small domestic possessions—the little things not covered by a will—be organized, decided upon, passed on? Naturally, I couldn't answer these questions. But from this dispassionate perspective, the viewpoint of the executor rather than the inhabitant, my apartment turned out to be a world of curiosities and enigmas, home reflected in a fun-house mirror, baffling and magical, full of abundance and deficit inextricably intertwined.

Back home in New York, I walked slowly around the house, mentally inventorying its contents. In the three-hundred-odd square feet of my apartment, I found that I had almost thirty yards of decorating fabric—chintzes, toiles, bright cottons—all uncut and unsewn; eleven pieces of needlepoint, unfinished by me or someone unknown; and four faded hooked rugs, none currently in use. My kitchen cabinets hold twenty sets of salt and pepper shakers, fourteen lumpy ceramic bowls, and twenty-three porcelain frogs. There are three colanders but no toaster, an iron but no ironing board, two full sets of dishes but no formal dining room table, and seven chairs, surely too many for the small space. I have no real stereo, only a tape deck the average preteen would be ashamed to own, but I own eight oil paintings—all old, all mediocre—and scores of old prints.

As I surveyed these things, I tried to pick up the thread

that tied these choices together. The lumpy bowls were the products of a friend fumbling toward mastery of the potter's wheel. The porcelain frogs were my grandmother's. These things were emblems of my connection to the people in my life; others witnessed my connection to the acts of thinking, looking, and making. I bought the bad paintings and flea market needlepoint canvases because I identified with their creators, and chose the chairs because I loved their hand-turned shapes and softly fading paint. The extra saltshakers, colanders, and plates were bought because each in its way symbolized human willingness to invest more effort in something than is strictly necessary—to decorate, to elaborate, to invent, to perfect.

My boxes of photographs and letters and my grand-mother's frogs help me fix myself within the resemblances and inheritances of a family tradition. My antiques link me to the larger continuities of an artistic one, like a dinghy firmly tied to the reassuring bulk of an ocean liner. For all their oddities, in fact, my possessions are the signs of my half-conscious attempt to shape, in my home and life, a satis-fying pattern, a redemptive narrative. Together, they con-struct a story in which I resemble my family but have grown beyond its limitations. In which I am loving and loved. In which I am buoyed up by, and not drowned in, the past. In which creativity is more potent than money or charm or luck, and in which the act of a person making something changes the world.

The story enacted in my home is shaped by the connections between the porcelain frogs and the wooden chairs, by the choice of the small paintings over the stereo, just as a poem or a novel is made not from words but from the intersections between them. But unlike a literary text, my apartment is unabashedly self-referential. It is a lullaby I sing to myself, my attempt to soothe my own worries, to quell my own fears.

In someone else's eyes, the abundances and deficits, the choices and priorities of this apartment may have no meaning. It may seem as irrational, as extreme to them as Jeanne's house did to me. In someone else's house the needlepoint rugs and the French headboard will become part of a separate pattern of affections and fears. I will be a minor or major character in that story, a beneficent or troubling model. But it won't be me that the story is told to solace; it won't be me whom it's invented to reassure.

And yet . . . I recently came across a book that explored eighteenth-century French interiors through the records left by Parisian probate inventories, made after death in cases where issues of inheritance were in dispute. The objects and materials listed in these records—the brocatelle and *droguet* fabrics, the beds *en tombeau* and *à la duchesse*—may be archaic, but their owners are not. Their preoccupations, pretensions, aspirations, and fears can be read from even these brief and partial household lists. A wealthy lawyer of Parlement, the book says, owned no mirrors, wall hangings, or curtains at the time he died, while a far less affluent maître d'hôtel possessed a marquetry clock, two paintings, a seven-section tapestry, a statue of Louis XIII, and a grandfather clock in a marquetry case of ebony and horn. The prosperous owner of a bookstore had not a single book in his home, but the wife of a stonecutter, leaving a modest estate, had fifty-eight prints under glass and seventeen paintings on wood when she died. One Madame Ollivier, a widow who died alone on the rue d'Anjou, lived in a small, single-room dwelling improbably packed with fifteen armchairs. A former quartermaster who died in 1748, "in the depths of misery" and with a paltry estate owned portraits of himself, his wife, and his daughter; together, these images "made up the sole decoration of his poor dwelling." These accounts of death and dispersal seemed almost unbearably poignant to me, moving rather than depressing as one might expect them to be. They attest to the vividness with which the priorities and affections of a particular human life can be communicated through the most apparently inconsequential of traces, the most ordinary and unself-conscious things.

❧ ☙

Jeanne died in the hospital the summer after that visit. I wasn't there for her death or her funeral. Ironically, I was sick myself, with a condition that a series of tests eventually labeled as "serious but treatable." The diagnosis was a happy resolution to a few anxious weeks. But the whole episode kept the specter of mortality on my mind, and—coupled with Jeanne's death—it reminded me again of that identification I'd felt with her for so many years.

On a visit to Florida soon afterward, I helped my parents with the complicated job of emptying Jeanne's house. As I helped organize Jeanne's books and tag her clothing for Goodwill, I found a closet full of size-six dresses she had not been small enough to wear for years, maybe decades. A shelf packed with books on wife swapping and swinging tucked behind the more impressive volumes devoted to history, art, sports, and sailing. Hundreds of carefully captioned photographs of the son and grandchildren in Oregon she had never in my memory taken the time to visit.

Again, as I had the year before, I caught glimpses of a self Jeanne had never willingly revealed, perhaps not even secretly acknowledged. The Jeanne reflected by her rooms was at once more romantic, more sexual, more obsessive, and more helpless than she had let on, or than I had imagined. I couldn't connect the woman I had known to the things she left—or even connect the things to one another. There was no story to be read in them. More accurately, maybe, there were too many stories, a dense tangle of narratives without a central theme or a single clear direction.

My parents and I packed the things Jeanne had given me so I could ship them home. As my mother and I cleaned and organized, I took a handful of other things as well, small things no one else wanted. A plump pottery mug I remembered her using; one of her husband, Harry's, military medals; a book on bird-watching; and a small object I found folded neatly in a dresser drawer among what looked like cherished mementos. I say "object" because I'm not quite sure what it is supposed to be. It's a pointy-nosed bear, or maybe a dog, crocheted of faded blue wool. It wears a bedraggled satin bow around its neck and has small white shirt-button eyes. A zipper runs up the front of its narrow, unstuffed torso, as though it is meant to hold something inside. It isn't a puppet or toy. If it has a function, I can't figure out what it is.

I took it on impulse, stuffing it into my pocket for reasons I couldn't have explained, finding room for it in my full suitcase, and propping it finally against the lamp on my desk, where it sits, floppy and ridiculous, as I write. I have no idea why Jeanne owned this little bear, or why she kept it so carefully. But I do know, by now, why I took it. Its mystery impelled me, the enigma of this particular thing being owned in this particular time by this particular woman. It goes with none of the Jeannes I know—not the confident, biting woman she seemed to be, and not the overwhelmed or obsessive one her house seems to have sheltered. I like the fact that I've inherited a little piece of this strangeness, this unaccountability, along with the more valuable legacies of writing table and lamp. I like the possibility that Jeanne might have been a little more like me—as sentimental, as secretly tenderhearted—than I'd come to think, even though I know that this is itself a sentimental hope.

The little blue bear is an extra link to the past and also to the future. Peculiar as it sounds, I like the idea of someone, someday, finding it as part of the inventory of my home after I am gone, and puzzling over where it fits in the life story of the woman memorialized by the saltshakers, china frogs, and handmade chairs—perhaps taking it home themselves, a small, ridiculous monument to the unknowable human soul.

Outside

Lately I've been dreaming about being outside: out of

my apartment, my building, my city. In one of these dreams

I'm stretched out, flat and relaxed, on the lawn of a shady

backyard. The thickness of the grass and the scent of black-eyed Susans signal late summer. The long shadows and cooling breeze tell of the moment when midday starts arcing into late afternoon. I lie looking at the canopy of trees above me, watching the sun shifting through the rustling leaves. In another of these dreams, I'm lying on the warm sand with the grey waves of the Atlantic breaking somewhere beyond my feet. The late afternoon sun is warm on my face, the wind shifting and cool. The air smells of salt and tar and suntan lotion. In both dreams I am still, peaceful, cradled in an afternoon that seems to last forever. And I know, somehow, that the ground on which I lie is mine, my possession, my turf, my property, my claim. There is no action in either dream, but I wake from them feeling that something has happened to me, that something significant has taken place.

When I am awake these dreams make me think of the houses of my New Jersey childhood. At my family's home in Caldwell I would sometimes spend the weekend's late afternoons—the shared tasks of the morning done, the family's members dispersed to their individual pleasures—lying on the lawn, looking up at the sky through the shivering oak branches. At my grandparents' house in Deal I spent those late afternoon hours on the bright still beach. But in the dreams themselves the time is always now and I am myself, an adult, a woman arcing into her own midafternoon. The dreams are about a future that gives me back things I no longer have and didn't even know I once again wanted. Connection, as tangible as the feeling of my shoulders against the grass or beach sand, with the earth. Rest. Ease. Quiet. A sense of possession, rootedness, ownership.

I rarely remember my dreams, and even more rarely turn to them for guidance. But the power and persistence of these makes me want to pay attention. I think they are signals—presentiments, maybe—about what is going to be the end of my life in New York as I have known it. About the end of my long assumption that this apartment and this city are the places where I must be, about the end of my desire to live in a tiny space and a huge metropolis. I'm not packing my things today, maybe not even tomorrow. The dreams are just that—promises or portents, not plans. They are just the first signs, I think, of a readiness that catches my conscious mind unaware: a readiness to move out and to move on.

❦

I have lived in the same apartment for almost thirteen years. In the year I chose it, Manhattan apartments were like bulbs at the height of tulip mania, costly and coveted. An electric current of hysteria seemed to run through the tenants and landlords of the city. People paid huge sums for dim, cramped spaces and were sensible to do it. The $300 in monthly rent I could afford to spend forced me to view illegal sublets, fifth-floor walk-ups with bathtubs in their kitchens, studios whose windows opened directly onto anonymous feet striding along the pavement. By the time I saw this apartment, I was desperate. It wasn't hard to persuade myself that its high ceilings and scuffed parquet floors had a modicum of attractiveness, at least a small measure of charm.

On the day I signed the lease, a broiling July Thursday, I picked up the keys, negotiated the building's gauntlet of locked security doors, stepped into my new hallway, and felt the bubble of my hopefulness burst. The air was stale and damp, the ceilings dingy, the walls scabrous with old paint. Outside the windows were the sad brick backs of other buildings, a rusted tangle of fire escapes, and, across the alley, a tarpaper-paved terrace on which an elderly man in an undershirt slept in a sagging yellow chair. I walked through the rooms seeing things I hadn't noticed the day before. The little pulley clothesline on the bathroom ceiling, from which a few clothespins still hung. The yellowed newspaper lining the kitchen cabinets. The sticky pleated paper frills tacked to the front edges of each shelf. The future this apartment promised wasn't the fast track of career success and romantic possibility I had hoped for. It was a life of difficult and decreasing choices, lived on the border between limitation and panic, an existence solitary and drab and somehow pathetic. I sat on the cool tile floor of the kitchen, my back against one wall and my feet propped against the other, and cried. I promised myself that I would move out as soon as I could, the minute my lease ran out or even sooner.

More than a decade later, I was still there. I stayed in the apartment for all sorts of good reasons: because the market was tight, because the market was dropping and it would be even cheaper to move next year, because I decided I'd rather invest my money in a trip to Europe or graduate school. Stranger than the simple fact of not moving is how little not moving surprised me. Everything else in my life was always up for grabs. My jobs, my friends, my interests, and my lovers changed, but never this small central place. Something in me fought hard and stealthily to stay where I was. Whatever it is, it has been powerful enough to make me forget that I feel confined in this apartment, that I am ambivalent about the city, that I once loved the shore and the cozy green hills of the not-quite-country. In my two persistent dreams, my psyche seems to be remembering some of these things, not just thinking about them but finally feeling them once more.

❧ ❧

When I was growing up, I was totally content with my house, yard, block, neighborhood, and town. I would never have believed you if you had told me that changing them could bring adventure or improvement. My family had moved into our house the year I turned three. Once our few boxes were unpacked, we settled in for the long run. Planting slow-growing spruce seedlings and replacing old pipes with durable copper ones, buying a new furnace, building in bookshelves and kitchen cabinets, my parents acted out an unconscious commitment to the house and its future. They never hesitated to invest time on projects with no immediate results, and even when the budget was tight, they found a way to afford the most enduring materials. It was worth it, their work and planning declared; we'll be here tomorrow. And we were. The baby blue spruce I planted myself when I was five blocked the sun from my second-story bedroom window by the time we moved out of the house.

The very idea of a family moving from house to house seemed alien to the world as I knew it. The neighborhood around us was a stable place, full of big houses built before the people who owned them were born and big families that seemed to extend endlessly in time, like a single, seamless generation. People sometimes moved in or out, but not so often that I noticed it. The Bateses' house was always the Bateses' house, the Learys' always the Learys'. We referred to the houses by family name rather than number, as though the residents were as inextricable from their home as snails from their shells. In neighborhood talk, the Corwins' house was still the Corwins' house twenty years after the Corwins themselves had moved on.

The continuity of my childhood was broken only when my grandparents moved out of that big, beloved shore house in Deal. Twelve at the time, I found myself in a kind of limbo: too young to really understand the adult calculations involved, and yet—in my mind, at least—too old to either admit to a sense of loss or demand consolation for it. I had assumed that my grandparents' house, like my own, would always be there for me. I had assumed I had a claim in it, a right, a kind of ownership. Their move proved that I was wrong and that I was powerless, that I had no control at all over this place that was so important to me. In the face of my sadness and anger I was helpless, mute, and even worse, ashamed.

The images of the move are jumbled in my mind. The baby grand piano that sat in the corner of the living room was unceremoniously humped down the green-painted front steps of the house and into the waiting van of its buyer. The beach towel that had always been mine, its white ground gaily patterned with seahorses, was rolled and packed and sealed up in a carton. Box after box was stuffed with newspaper-wrapped shapes and marked with my grandmother's precise Palmer script. The blank row of the house's front windows was suddenly stripped naked, ugly without the graceful shading of their Austrian blinds. It seemed to me that the house virtually bled familiar objects, that rugs and pictures and bric-a-brac spilled out of the front door like blood from an unstanchable wound.

No one else seemed to share my anger or my grief, not even my grandmother, who, I knew, loved the house and its stable peacefulness as much as I did. It made me angry, this silent obedience. I didn't understand that her loyalty was to her husband, not her house; I began to learn that female adulthood did not necessarily bring with it power or control. My grandmother complied with my grandfather, doing what she did not want to do with an air of stoic cheerfulness. I complied, too, watching without protest, playing the good girl's role, concealing what seemed to be the selfish intensity of my emotions—fury, loss, fear—under a mask of sensible obedience.

No one in our family made any formal acknowledgment of the move. There were no rituals, no ceremonies, no family talks, no gestures: no gathering of cuttings to be rerooted in a new garden, no giving of small gifts or mementos, no carving of names on a windowsill or tree. I didn't understand then that this is a failing of my family, a skill or gift we do not have. We were—and are—good at rituals of celebration, of arrival, of achievement. We are less good at ceremonies of mourning, of departure, of loss. We pretend these changes away by working furiously on the practical tasks of planning and packing, and we vent our sadness haphazardly, in small and petty disputes.

❧ ❧

My family still lived in Caldwell when I went away to college. It was my first real stay away from my parents. But I moved into my freshman dorm, then into my sophomore one, then into the off-campus apartments of my junior and senior years, without problems. I was proud of my own composure and good cheer, my own capable maturity. My parents were pleased as well. We had managed this transition the way we all liked best, as if it were a simple business transaction. It was, we all said in delight, as though nothing had changed. It didn't occur to us that in some sense nothing had—that I had not so much left home as simply set up temporary camp.

This is common to college kids—nothing strange. But even when I moved into Manhattan and the apartment I live in today, the house in Caldwell was still the place I instinctively called home. The unsettling and scary parts of life in the apartment and the city were buffered by my sense—not quite conscious—that it was not wholly or really my life. Like a seedling that falls only as far as the soft soil between its parents' roots, I grew and changed but remained dependent, unrooted in my own home ground.

When I look at the engagement diaries for my first years in New York, it's the weekdays that seem full, dense with scribbled notes of dinners out, evening classes, dates, visits to galleries or plays. The weekends are almost always blank. Sometimes there is a brief note, a reference to a museum visit or a stay in the Hamptons. More often there is nothing, or just the single laconic word "home," still a reference to Caldwell. The essential parts of my life were marked by those calm empty spaces.

Those weeks really started on Friday nights, with the slow meandering arc of the DeCamp bus going west along Route 46. It dropped me off on Caldwell's main street, and if the weather was clear, I walked the two blocks up the hill to home, a walk familiar from decades of childhood trips to school, to church, to the toy and candy stores of town. There had been some changes since my childhood. The Learys had moved, old Mr. Bates had died, and there was a new family in the once-decrepit shingle cottage on the corner. But the houses themselves, the big old trees, and most of the people I met were the same. After the liveliness of New York, Caldwell seemed hushed and still, as though it had been fixed in the amber of time. Maybe that's why I remember those walks as if every one of them were lit with the sharply slanted golden sun of the late summer's long evening; as if it were always that moment when daylight is lingering long beyond its time, poignant and miraculous.

I didn't do much during those weekends. That was part of their attraction, the way they let me be as unself-consciously aimless as a child. I walked the dog, took naps, went with my father to the garden center and with my mother to the deli, sat on the front porch looking at the sunset or the rain, visited the few high school friends who hadn't left town. I worked too hard—on housecleaning, gardening, or whatever renovation project my father had going—to be a mere guest. But the work, even when it was tiring, had the ease of tasks that carry no real responsibility with them. Over lunch or dinner I told my parents and sister about my busy week in New York, about my job and my dates and my forays into New York's cultural scene. I didn't tell them how anxious and lonely that life would have been without the corrective of those intervals at home, simply because those healing weekends allowed me not to see it.

❧

Five years after I rented my apartment, my parents went to Florida for an ordinary vacation and came back with the blueprints for a house already under construction. All of us children were grown by this time, but my parents hadn't talked to us before they'd made their decision. Maybe they knew that to explain their thoughts—to solicit opinions, to debate the pros and cons, to consider the move at length—would have made it impossible for them to go. Maybe they were simply overtaken, in the balmy Florida air, by an urgent need to free themselves from my father's exhausting job, the endless work on the house, or the cold New Jersey winters.

With a sort of grim precision, the next ten months reprised my grandparents' move more than a decade before. The abruptness of the decision and the protracted labor of the move; my helplessness, which itself felt shameful; the lack of any ceremony or closure—all of this felt horribly familiar. Even now our departure from the Caldwell house feels at once too raw and too distanced to talk about evenly. I am not sure who I was during this time or who my parents were, and like that of my grandparents, this move stays in my memory only as a tumble of disconnected images and emotions.

My last leisured, unself-conscious weekend at my childhood home was the weekend before my parents announced their move. Visits after that felt heavy with unsayable things. The still, clear waters of my home life in Caldwell were suddenly turbulent and muddied, full of undercurrents. I thought at the time that I was the only one to feel this, though I no longer believe this is true.

My parents, particularly my father, seemed to want a wholehearted approval from me that I was too grief stricken to give. He could not seem to understand how divided I was between love and sadness, how I could at once sincerely want the best for him and grieve fiercely, almost angrily, for my own lost home. Looking back from a safe distance, it is easier to see how defensive this must have made him feel. About my mother I am even less sure. As I had with my grandmother, I somehow expected her to play mediator, redeemer, champion of the house and of domestic continuity. She didn't, and probably couldn't.

I never really said good-bye to the house. I managed no rituals or ceremonies of departure on my own. I put off packing my things and making arrangements for their storage until the last minute, ensuring that my final visits would be too busy to be sad, buried in an avalanche of jobs I could put off no longer. I saw the house for the last time through the angled rearview mirror of a rented car laden with beloved possessions hastily loaded and stacked, and though I have passed very close to Caldwell on trips to New Jersey and Pennsylvania, I have never gone back.

❧ ❧

With the sale of the Caldwell house, I lost the privilege of living with one foot still planted on the safe ground of my childhood, solidly on the terra firma of my own past. I found myself standing in a present I didn't entirely like. Suddenly I was accountable for making my own home, creating my own leisure. I didn't like the feeling, though it turned out to be one of the hidden gifts my parents' move gave me.

For the first time in my life, the word "home" had no single definition, referred to no single, primal place. Sometimes when I used the word, I was referring to my New York apartment, sometimes to my parents' house in Florida. The distinction did not feel very important. Both uses of it feel comfortable, but neither is invested with magical authority or eternal rightness.

My parents have ended up living in the same Florida town as my grandparents. It bears no resemblance to Caldwell. The community is a transient one, filled with older couples who spend the summer up north and younger ones with short-term leases; change is an affirmation, not a betrayal, of the nature of the place, and nothing to get excited about. There are attractive houses and ugly ones, but there is no sense of innate union between them, their residents, the land. As I drive up the street to my parents' house, neither time nor the light are miraculously halted. I enjoy the visits, but they are no longer mystical returns.

❧ ❧

Last night I dreamed again of lying in that green backyard. As I woke, I thought I could still smell the moistness of the soil and hear the sleepy buzzing of the yellow jackets in the garden. Once I was finally fully awake, I realized something new about these dreams, recognized suddenly the void that is at the center of them and that makes them feel so new and so powerful.

At the heart of both dreams is an absence. No house, no man-made enclosure at all, is visible in them. This central symbol of my life and of my writing, to which I return time and time again, is entirely missing.

Images of being outside, excluded even temporarily from home, have always been anxious ones for me, symbols of displacement and fear and discomfort. But in these dreams the fact that I am outside doesn't mean that I'm homeless, wandering, lost, losing. I'm peaceful in them, and unafraid, and confident in the claim I've somehow staked on my particular place. I'm safe in the world outside the home, rocked and warmed and enclosed within its openness. It does not feel to me as though the house has disappeared or been lost for good. It feels as though it is somewhere behind me, as though it can be taken for granted, as though it stands, sufficient and enduring, somewhere just beyond the boundary of my sight.

Acknowledgments

Richard Locke read the first of these essays in draft form and saw a book there; I am profoundly grateful for his generosity, belief, and vision, without which this book could never have been written. Special thanks also to Herbert Leibowitz, who helped a fledgling essayist hone her skills, and to Paul DeAngelis, who thought I'd be a writer a very long time before I was.

Some of these pieces carry dedications to those who inspired them or made them possible. "Kitchen" is for Patricia Fox, "Entrance Hall Two" for Saul Fox, and "Dining Room" for Marie Dougherty; "Entrance Hall One" is dedicated to the memory of Joseph Howard Dougherty, Jr. "Playroom" is for Victoria Donnelly and Andrew Fox, and "Children's Room" is for the younger generation: Olivia, Matthew, Nathaniel, and Katherine. "Inside" is for Betsy Chabot and Doug Manley; "Bedroom One" for Eileen McGurn; "Guest

Room" for Sheryl Conkleton and Joseph Newland; and "Outside" for Joan Kavanaugh, with profound appreciation.

I am especially grateful to my agent, Wendy Lipkind; to Cindy Gitter; to Jennifer O'Grady, an unswervingly steady and lucid presence; to Anna Rabinowitz, for her generous assistance; and to Judy Sund, source of great conversation and endless art historical help. Warmest thanks also to Thelma Adams, Elizabeth Childs, Sylvia Foley, Hope Hanafin, Brenda Hussen, Carole Jacobs, the Judson Institute, John Kavanaugh, Marion Maneker, Grafton Nunes, Sherie Posesorski, Sandi Rygiel, and Beth Tueller; to years of Tuesday night companions, too numerous to name here but none the less greatly appreciated; and to the faculty and staff of the Columbia University School of the Arts.

Final revisions to this book were made during a residency at the Corporation of Yaddo, whose support I gratefully acknowledge.

Notes

Jean-François Bastide's novel *La Petite Maison*, which I quote in "Bedroom Two," is translated and quoted at some length in John Whitehead's *The French Interior in the Eighteenth Century* (New York: Dutton Studio Books, 1993).

"Dining Room's" references to the history of living alone come from Beatrice Gottlieb's *The Family in the Western World from the Black Death to the Industrial Age* (New York: Oxford University Press, 1993). The letter quoted appears in May Sarton's *Journal of a Solitude* (New York: Norton, 1973).

Philippe Ariès's *Centuries of Childhood: A Social History of Family Life* (New York: Alfred A. Knopf, 1962) provided background information for "Children's Room." Julian Schnabel's apartment was pictured in *House and Garden's* July 1985 issue, in an article written by Doris Saatchi. Information on modern rooms for children was taken from Pamela Scurry's *Cradle and All* (New York: Clarkson Potter, 1992), Annie Sloan and Felicity Bryan's *Nursery Style* (Chicago: Chicago Contemporary Books, 1989), and *The Better Homes and Gardens Book of Interior Design* (Des Moines: Better Homes and Gardens Books, 1987). The German prince's room was reproduced in Charlotte Gere's *Nineteenth-Century Decoration: The Art of the Interior* (New York: Harry N. Abrams, 1989). Susan Lasdun's *Victorians at Home* (New York: Viking Press, 1981) was a source on the function of the Victorian nursery.

In "Sickroom," the information on French estates is taken from Annik Pardailhe-Galabrun's *The Birth of Intimacy: Privacy and Domestic Life in Early Modern Paris* (Cambridge, Mass.: Polity Press, 1991).

Three other sources were also useful to me as I wrote this book. Together, Mario Praz's *Interior Decoration from Pompeii to Art Nouveau* (New York: Thames and Hudson, 1982) and Peter Thornton's *Authentic Decor: The Domestic Interior 1620–1920* (New York: Viking Press, 1984) offered hundreds of thought-provoking reminders of the many faces of domestic life. Finally, Witold Rybczynski's *Home* (New York: Viking Press, 1986) provided an insightful and invaluable perspective on the history of the home.

Out of respect for their privacy, I have changed the names and identifying details of some of the people spoken of in this book.

ABOUT THE AUTHOR

Suzanne Fox has a B.A. in art history and an M.F.A. from Columbia University. A freelance writer, she divides her time between New York City and Vero Beach, Florida.